We Armenians Survived!

Battle of Marash 1920

Ellen Sarkisian Chesnut

Andrew Benzie Books
Martinez, California

Published by Andrew Benzie Books
www.andrewbenziebooks.com

Printed in the United States of America
First Edition: November 2019, Revised March 2020

10 9 8 7 6 5 4 3 2 1

Chesnut, Ellen Sarkisian
We Armenians Survived!
The Battle of Marash 1920

ISBN: 978-1-7330159-0-5

Library of Congress Catalog Number: *Pending*

Cover and book design by Andrew Benzie
www.andrewbenziebooks.com

This book is dedicated to my mother, Evelyn,
and my grandmother, Heranoush.
Both women throughout their lives confronted adversity
head on and were noted for their humor and resilience.

CONTENTS

ACKNOWLEDGEMENTS

Thanks first and always to all the families and persons mentioned in this book for their invaluable help and support in making the stories of our parents and more becoming known and continuing to be known.

Specifically (in chronological order of book), THANKS TO:

Marlene Griffith Bagdikian who gave me permission to use pages 165-183 from *The Memoir of Lydia Bagdikian* edited by Ben Bagdikian, Lydia's younger brother and Marlene's husband (now deceased). Also, thanks to Marlene for permission to use the Bagdikian family photo found on page "v" in *The Memoir of Lydia Bagdikian*.

Telma Trimmer nee Berberian (Dicran Berberian's niece) and her husband, **Robert Whitfield Trimmer, PhD** for permission to use the papers of Dicran Abraham Berberian, MD that was given to them in 1973.

Raff Berberian (son of Dicran Berberian & my second cousin) for permission to use *A Remembrance of My Parents: Dicran and Armine Berberian*, written 1988.

Cynthia Berberian Hale (daughter of Dicran Berberian & my second cousin) for her unswerving support of this project, use of photographs of her parents and grandparents, and for connecting me to my relatives **Vahe Nalbandian** and his sister **Keghany** who have forwarded data (of births and deaths) found on sheets of paper removed from a very old Nalbandian bible.

Dikran Yepremian, my Armenian Language Teacher, who helped with the translation of the data from the Nalbandian bible which was written in Turkish using the Armenian alphabet.

Nancy Joyce Yeranian-Haig (my cousin) for permission to use Chapter 6, "A True Story," from her father, Arthur S. Yeranian's book, *The Civilized*.

Margaret Elaine Shamlian (my cousin) who researched the life of her father, Puzant Shamlian and grandfather Hagop Shamlian and for sending me valuable information about our grandfather, "an unsung hero of Marash."

Arlene Shamlian Kazarian (my aunt, deceased) who mailed me, in 2015, photocopies of the written recollections of her cousin, Dr. Dicran Berberian.

Dennis Shamlian (my cousin) for his own recollections of his father Edward, and mother Araxie (Roxie) and for photographs of their wedding.

Janet Shamlian Ishkanian (my cousin) for her own recollections of her father Edward and Mother Araxie (Roxie) and her permission to use her eulogy given at the funeral service of our aunt Arlene Shamlian Kazarian.

Linda Shamlian Force (my cousin) for the tribute to her father, Toros Shamlian (my uncle), about his remarkable life.

David Kherdian (poet) and **Garig Basmadjian** (poet) who both translated the poem by Yeghishe Charentz, "There are Invisible Guests" which concludes this book.

And THANKS TO the following for their interest, support, and expertise that have gone into this book:

Ara Ghazarians, PhD, curator of the Armenian Cultural Foundation in Arlington, MA for taking time away from his heavy schedule to read the book and offer suggestions to make it better.

Sharon B. Murphy, musician, who took time away from her music to type the initial versions of this book.

Ramya Srinivasan, Independent Editor for editing the book. Her suggestions and expertise were of invaluable help to me.

ELLEN SARKISIAN CHESNUT
FAMILY TREE

great-grandma
ISGOUHI RUBIAN SHAMLIAN
1847-1916

great-grandma
first name unknown
NALBANDIAN

great-grandpa
TOROS SHAMLIAN
1840-1904

great-grandpa
HAGOP NAI RANDIAN
1837-1910

grandma
HERANOUSH NALBANDIAN SHAMLIAN
1882-1956

grandpa
HAGOP SHAMLIAN
1866-1960

mom
EVELYN SHAMLIAN SARKISIAN
1910-1983

great-grandma
first name unknown
KUPJIAN

great-grandpa
first name unknown
KUPJIAN

great-grandma
first name unknown
MESROBIAN

great-grandpa
first name unknown
MESROBIAN

grandma
HATUN KUPJIAN MESROBIAN
?-1915

grandpa
MARKAR MESROBIAN
?-1915

dad
"DELI" SARKIS SARKISIAN
1905-1995

me
ELLEN SARKISIAN CHESNUT

Krikor Shamlian—Great Great Grandfather of the SHAMLIAN FAMILY was born in 1750 in Damascus, Syria and died in 1797 in Marash, Turkey. He came to Marash in 1775. Krikor had an Arab relative in Damascus by the name of Habib. SHAM in Arabic means Demascus.

My father, "Deli" Sarkis was a member of the MESROBIAN clan, the largest family group in KERAMET village in Turkey (Bursa Province). After the Genocide of 1915-1923 when almost all MESROBIANS were killed off, my father began using MARKARIAN as his last name, in honor of his father, Markar. Subsequently, however-er, my father created a new name for himself, "Deli" Sarkis Sarkisian and a new identity.

5

INTRODUCTION

One hundred and four years after the GREAT CRIME—the Armenian Genocide of 1915-1923—real justice remains elusive for the perpetrators (in Turkey) and for the victims (now spread world-wide): both long deceased.

The Battle of Marash in 1920 and the burning and destruction of the city of Smyrna in 1922 were the last of the conflagrations in the Turkish struggle for independence from 1919-1923 led by Mustafa Kemal (aka Ataturk).

In both Marash and Smyrna, many innocent Armenians and other Christian people were subjected to unimaginable levels of hatred, brutality, and violence by Turks in Smyrna and by both Turks and Kurds in Marash. Yet, in Turkey today, the victims do not even warrant so much as a footnote in the governmental revisionist history of the period from 1915 to 1923. The victims are depicted as guilty of atrocities and the perpetrators as their innocent victims: a classic example of inversion. This falsehood is one of the driving forces behind my writing of this book. Eyewitnesses were there on the ground such as my mother, her parents, her siblings, and countless others among them. That is why their recollections play such an important part in this book.

My grandfather, Hagop Shamlian, had to get out of Marash during the battle since the major Turkish leaders of Marash had fifty gold pounds on his head. Why you ask? It was the time of World War I and during this period he was instrumental in saving scores of Armenian men and boys from deportation to remote, unknown regions: he was an Armenian Schindler, so to speak. Since he was not given to self-aggrandizement and only told his immediate family what he had done, his deeds are only now being brought out to the community at large in this book.

Grandfather Hagop's recollections of the abandonment of the city of Marash in 1920 by French forces, who were then followed by 3,000 Armenians, are skimpy at best as his family did not record his day to day travails on the four to five day trek out of Marash. Therefore, I have relied on the memoir of Lydia Bagdikian—*The Memoir of Lydia Bagdikian: A Childhood in Two Countries*—to fill in the gaps. Lydia Bagdikian was ten years old in 1920 and was in the same group of refugees as my grandfather. The two chapters from her memoir, which she wrote as a grown woman, give us an idea of what it was like in the blizzard conditions that 3,000 Armenians withstood trekking out of Marsh for the last time.

There are also the possible recollections on tapes my grandfather and others made in the 1940s that may help add to the understanding of these survivor's experiences during the turbulent and violent times during and after World War I in Turkey and the Near East. However, these are "lost tapes!". Why?

I received a note dated February 23, 1989 from Janice Vagim Barigian, the granddaughter of Ferideh Vagim my grandfather Hagop's sister. Janice wrote me of the comments made by her aunt Blanche Vagim the second wife of Ed Vagim who was Ferideh's eldest son:

> "My Aunt Blanche Vagim would like to have Toros Shamlian's address. She has some audiotapes that Toros, Ed Vagim and Hagop and Mr. Dishian made. She would like Toros to have them."

The tapes had been made in Fresno, California in 1941 when all of the Shamlians were reunited. Later, when I got in touch with Doug Vagim, Ed Vagim's son, he told me that the tapes were given to Fresno State; and, he would tell me nothing more. I do not know what those tapes contained; therefore, their relevance to my family's personal history and the events in Marash is unknown.

As for the seed of this book, it began in the mid-1980s, when I began to interview relatives on both sides of my family. I bought the book *The Lions of Marash* by Dr. Stanley E. Kerr, who was an officer in the United States Army Sanitation Corps during WWI. He originally served in Aleppo in different positions, including clinical biochemist and photographer. He came to Marash in the autumn of 1919. The Battle of Marash ensued in 1920. Years later, Kerr wrote *The Lions of Marash*, which included, not only his own experiences during 1920 and afterwards, but those of French officers, priests, Turkish military historians, and Armenian survivors of the annihilation of Armenian civilians during the battle.

Kerr heroically worked to recover Armenian children in Marash who had forcibly been taken into Turkish and Kurdish homes. When the French withdrew from Marash in the winter of 1920, Kerr took charge of American relief operations. During the same time as my interviews with relatives, I learned of another book related to Marash called: *Dust to Destiny*. It tells the story of Tamam Zarouhi Getsoyan, a teacher in Marash. I immediately notified Arthur Yeranian, (married to my aunt Rebecca) who had as a child gone to school in Marash. He wrote me back on September 10, 1988:

> "Dear Ellen: What you sent me recently was a real surprise. Thank you. Back in 1915 or 1916, I guess, I was a student in the kindergarten of the German Orphanage School but commuting from home to school every school day. I recall that a 'she-teacher' by the name of Tamam was also my teacher that year. We used to call her 'Tamam Varchuhi' (Teacher TAMAM). I'm fairly certain this person is the same one. Thank you again."

I further discovered another valuable book that detailed what it was like in Marash during those trying years between 1914-1922 called *Neither To Laugh Nor to Weep* by Abraham H. Hartunian. Reverend Hartunian was the pastor of The First Armenian Evangelical Church: the same church where my grandfather, Hagop Shamlian, had been a member. In the book, Hartunian speaks of

Reverend Abraham Berberian, who was the clergyman of the newly formed Turkish Christian Church; subsequently, the handwritten memoirs of Abraham Berberian's son, Dicran, come to play an important role in my book. Reverend Hartunian also knew Arthur Yeranian's uncle, Hagop Yeranian, who during the Genocide of 1915-1916 had been deported to Marash from Afion Kara-Hissar and had led a prayer meeting at Hartunian's church. Hagop Yeranian's life unfortunately ended in Smyrna in 1922 when he collapsed and died trying to escape the inferno set by the Turks.

*   *   *

It is absolutely unbelievable to me that the Armenians of the Ottoman Empire persisted in leading such normal lives as they could, even when they were subjected to one genocide after the other. What better way to live a normal life than to raise and educate the young? Father Derhayr Gorun Shrikian, (see bibliography), writes of the centers of learning established by American educators and missionaries throughout the Ottoman Empire. The chapter that interested me the most was of course the one about Marash.

In 1866, a seminary was opened with the goal of educating young men to serve as pastors and preachers in the evangelical churches of the Central Turkey Mission. Then, in 1904, a Girls' College building was erected in Marash. Its purpose was to train girls to become teachers, do field work, and eventually become good Christian mothers. There were also several boys' high-school academies that prepared young men to further their education at the Central Turkey College and at St. Paul's Institute at Tarsus. According to Derhayr Shrikian, many students of the Armenian Apostolic faith studied at these Protestant schools and later became respected intellectuals and educators who served Armenian communities throughout the Ottoman Empire.

*   *   *

Marjorie Housepian Dobkin, an Armenian historian, countered the denial of the genocide by successive governments in Turkey with a statement that many others and I have taken to heart: "No amount of money and propaganda disguised as scholarship will succeed in changing the historical record."

Umit Kurt, a scholar born in Aintab, a once-thriving Armenian community, has taken upon himself the task of exposing what really happened during the years 1895-1922. Kurt posted an especially informative paper on Academia.edu called "The Curious Case of Ali Cenani Bey (1872-1934) from Aintab." It revealed that the masterminds of the Genocide were not the common ordinary Turks and Kurds but were the "elites" like Ali Cenani Bey.

Kurt writes about the astronomical losses to Armenians between 1895 and 1922—loss of life and property being just two of these major losses. Kurt further details the techniques utilized in 1915 to streamline the confiscation of wealth: "mass executions of Armenian elites, followed by categorical deportations, forced assimilation, destruction of material culture, and collective dispossession."

When the Armenian survivors of the forced deportations from Turkey of 1915-1916 began returning in 1919 (following Turkey's defeat in WWI) to their villages and cities in Cilicia—which included Aintab and Marash—the Turkish elites were nervous. And, they did everything they could to finish off the Armenians once and for all. They were not about to return Armenian wealth, and they didn't. Umit Kurt states, "The perpetrators and their families profited from the genocide to the extent that, after 1923, entire generations were educated and supported by the 'start-up' capital of Armenian property acquired in 1915."

We Armenians Survived! The Battle of Marash, 1920 is an unbelievable story of luck and persistence. The Armenians whose stories are told here knew that their lives were indeed gifts, as so many around them lost theirs. How different from the humble, self-effacing memoirs in this book are the over 200 memoirs written by Turkish perpetrators of the Armenian Genocide. No effort is made to deny the atrocities committed. Armenians were thought of as the enemy, as vermin, as disease, as not human, and above all it was of military necessity to be rid of them all. There seems no moral introspection on the part of any of these perpetrators, many of whom went to their deaths with no remorse. They thought their acts of destruction would create something radiantly new. They were wrong! The only ones who created something radiantly new were the Armenians who fled the land of persecution, humiliation, and death. They ventured forth to lands where opportunity and freedom awaited them. This is their story.

CHAPTER 1
THE BLOODY EARTH, 1894-1923

As a ten year old, I was mesmerized by stories of heroic girls and women, whether they appeared in comic books like Wonder Woman or in the twelve collections of fairy tales otherwise known as Andrew Lang's *Fairy Books of Many Colors*. The more complicated and difficult the tasks faced by the heroine, the better! I had such a feeling of satisfaction after reading each story: I felt I was the one who saved everybody.

You can imagine my frustration as I listened to my mother's accounts of life as an Armenian in Marash, Turkey where she was born in 1910. Sadly, there was no happy ending for the Armenians in the city of her birth.

Marash is inland from the northeastern Mediterranean and 97 miles from Adana, Turkey. You'll find it on a current map as Kahramanmaras, or Heroic Marash. The setting is beautiful, nestled on the southern slope of the mountain Akhur Dagh which peaks at 8,000 feet. The valley and the inhabited areas of the slopes range from 1,500 to 3,000 feet of Akhur Dagh which is part of the Taurus chain of mountains in Cilicia. The area of Cilicia has been occupied since 2000 B.C.E. Hittites, Romans, Byzantines, Muslim Arabs, Crusaders, Armenians, and Turks controlled Marash throughout the centuries. The people were surrounded by historical castles, fortresses, and sculptures. The most famous were the sculptures discovered in 1883 of the Lions of Marash. One lion with hieroglyphic inscription was found in the citadel of Marash and a second uninscribed lion near one of the fortress gates. These lions were created during the reign of the ruler Halparuntiyas III at the end

13

of the 9th century BCE. He was the king of the Neo-Hittite kingdom of Gurgun that had its capital in the location of modern day Kahramanmaras (Marash).

Prior to 1915, the population of Marash was predominately Turks, Armenians, and Kurds. Before World War I, the population of Marash was estimated to be 65,000 people. Of this number, about 30,000 were Armenians. In the neighboring villages (Zeitoun, Findijak, Yarpouz, Albustan, and many other smaller villages) lived another 35,000-40,000 Armenians.

The idyllic setting of Marash masked horrific events that transpired in the latter years of the nineteenth century. I learned while speaking with my mother of how the Armenians of Marash and surrounding cities, towns, and villages had been subjected to one blood bath after another during the years 1894 through 1923.

The "Red Sultan", Abdulhamid II, played a pivotal role in ordering the massacres that began in 1894. He was the religious and political head of the Ottoman Empire and consequently, the Turkish Muslim population unquestioningly obeyed the Sultan since disobedience meant death.

European dignitaries who visited the palace of the sultan were dazzled by the splendor of his court with its luxurious appointments, inventions, and toys. They would soon discover, however, the anti-Christian bias of this leader when terrible atrocities against Armenians were reported from the provinces. Abdulhamid's agents went into Western Armenia and deliberately fermented religious fanaticism among the local Muslim groups, whether they were Turks or Kurds.

One of Abdulhamid's most prized possessions was his telegraph machine which he kept under lock and key in his palace. It was an exceptionally useful means of communication when he ordered the massacre of Armenians to begin. It was also under his administration that an intelligence service was established with spies everywhere (many of whom were German). These spies secretly infiltrated Christian communities and sent messages back to the sultan. It is important to note that Abdulhamid later handed all of this information to the new head of the government, Talaat Pasha, who was the person directly responsible for the Genocide of 1915 against the Armenians.

Just as quickly as orders were sent out from the Sultan for a massacre to begin, he would send out another one for the atrocities to stop—oftentimes ending with the Turks and Kurds sheepishly going about their daily endeavors as if nothing happened. The following is an eyewitness account by Ephraim K. Jernazian, a survivor of the massacre in Marash that took place on November 18, 1895, who wrote this years later, remembering the experiences of his barely five-year-old self indelibly etched into his memory:

> "The Turks did come—very soon—while we were still praying. The mob chopped down our front door and three soldiers with guns, bolting up the stairs, broke into the room, glowering fiercely without asking any questions. One pointed his gun directly at Dicran Samuel stood up, stepped in front of Dicran, and pleaded, 'Kill me if you have to but spare my brother. He has a wife and a baby to look after.' Dicran jumped aside and forward saying, 'My brother is very young. Give him a chance. Kill me if you must.' The scowling intruders retorted, 'Don't worry. It's no problem. We will kill you both.' As the fatal shots rang out, I saw only two brothers collapse, lifeless onto the floor."[1]

For twelve years, from 1896 until April 1909, the Armenians who had survived the Hamidian massacres of 1894-1896 struggled to rebuild their homes, businesses, churches, and schools. Many missionaries already there and those newly arrived helped with the rebuilding of communities. Orphanages were established and work provided for Armenian widows, especially in the areas of needle lace, as the women were already very proficient in needle art. The money they earned would sustain their families and themselves.

The Turks and Kurds were astonished that the Armenians, whom they had tried so mightily to destroy (200,000 killed with 500,000 left homeless), had picked themselves up and had started anew. One member of my family was not so optimistic about the future for

Armenians in Turkey. That person was my maternal great-grandfather, Toros Shamlian. He had been born in Marash in 1840 and died on July 7, 1904 of cholera. Toros was christened by Nahabed der Garabedian in the Karasoun Manoog Church. However, some years later, he became a protestant. Toros married Isgouhi Rubian in 1862 with Reverend Avedis Poladian officiating. Isgouhi was a kind and loving woman and a tremendous helpmate to her husband. Toros was a pioneer in farming and a master shoemaker. He learned the trade in Aleppo and tanned leather from 1888 to 1890.

The situation after the Hamidian Massacres was precarious for those Armenians who wanted to reclaim their homes confiscated by the Turks and Kurds because of deep-seated Muslim hostility toward the Christian Armenians. Toros knew it was urgent to get his sons, Arsen and Garabed, along with his nephews, out of Turkey. His sister, Margaret Shamlian Geyikian who was born in Marash in 1843, felt the same. There's a photograph of Margaret and the Shamlian young men in America that was taken after their arrival in 1896 that was a treasured keepsake for years by family members who remained behind.

My grandfather, Hagop, did not go to America, as his father, Toros, needed him to run the tannery in Marash.

By 1908, the populace of the Ottoman Empire, both Muslim and Christian, were fed up with the harsh and arbitrary rule of the Sultan Abdulhamid. The Committee of Union and Progress [CUP] appeared as an alternative—seemingly a progressive advocate of democracy but cleverly hiding its true colors, since they proved to be even more repressive than the Sultan, and for the Armenians, far worse.

However, in 1908, the mood was celebratory, as the Armenians throughout the Ottoman Empire thought they had reason to rejoice since the government of the tyrant Abdulhamid II was overthrown. Many Armenians stood side by side next to the members of the CUP. They thought they would have the same rights as Muslims and would be able to overthrow the yoke of second-class citizenship or dhimmitude. They were foolish to think that the Muslim Turks would ever grant Christian Armenians, or any of the other minorities, equality under the law. The Turks would teach the Armenians a lesson for even contemplating such a change from the status quo. First, they would accuse the Armenians of revolting against the government: this manufactured accusation spread like wildfire. And, in early April of 1909 for ten or twelve days and nights, the largely unarmed Armenian population of Adana was literally put to the torch. As the esteemed historian of the Armenian Genocide, Vahakn N. Dadrian, stated: "It was one of the most gruesome and savage bloodbaths ever recorded in human history."

It was started first by the counter revolutionary forces of Sultan Abdulhamid who were joined by the army of the CUP who had been sent to Adana to quell the violence. Instead, they joined in the slaughter, all the while spreading the lie that the Armenians were revolting. The Muslim Turks and Kurds went into a frenzy of butchery. The results were 30,000 Armenian died and countless lives were destroyed.

Armenians did not remain silent. A doctor and a poet responded to the Adana massacre. Dr. Dicran Balakian was with a team of physicians and relief workers who went to the epicenter of the horrible events in Adana to treat the survivors. Dr. Balakian was stunned at what he witnessed and wrote letters to his relatives back home in Constantinople. A friend of the family, the poet Adom Yarjanian (pen name Siamanto) read the letters. He would not remain silent and transformed Balakian's testimonies into some of the most powerful poems of the twentieth century. So many Armenian lives in Adana were extinguished by torture and fire. Siamanto's poem, "The Dance," is narrated by a German woman. She is in a room, nursing a woman who has been stabbed and is dying. From her window she hears filthy songs. Going to the balcony of her window, she sees a crowd of men around a group of twenty Armenian females, stripped naked, who are being whipped as a man shouts at them, "You must dance." The women hold onto one another's hands and begin their circle dance. All the while obscenities are being hurled at them. As they fall, the crowd screams for them to get up. Then, someone brings a jug of kerosene and with a torch the naked "brides" are set on fire:

"And the charred bodies rolled and tumbled to their deaths. I slammed my shutters, sat down next to my dead girl and asked, 'How can I dig out my eyes?'"[2]

Zabel Yessayan was another witness to the aftermath of the Adana Massacre of 1909. She was with a group of relief workers sent to Adana from the headquarters of the Armenian Church in Constantinople. Yessayan was already a well known author, translator, and publicist. Like Dr. Balakian, she was shaken by the enormity of the destruction and its effect on the survivors. She spoke with women who were so broken psychologically that there was no way they could care for their children. She would also make sure that people learned about what had happened and wrote a searing book about the tragic fate of the Armenians called *In the Ruins*. It was published in Constantinople in 1911.

Another advocate for the Armenian victims was Krikor Zohrab, a writer, an influential journalist, an educator, and an internationally respected jurist. As a member of the Deputies of the Ottoman Parliament, he documented what happened in Hamidiye, which was in the province of Adana. Apparently, there was sharing of information about the beginning of the April 1, 1909 massacre. The Turks, by telegram, called up the neighboring Kurds to take part in the killings. It commenced a few hours later and was encouraged by the local mufti (a Muslim legal expert) empowered to give rulings on religious matters. The mufti, Sari Mehmed, called upon the Muslim believers to be harsh and merciless: 'Spare no one older than two years of age; if you want to save bullets, use axes,' he urged."[3]

In Adana, Armenians were once again blamed for the atrocities committed against them. However, Krikor Zohrab countered the accusations in the parliament against the Armenians and blamed the Adana Massacres on the government and local authorities. Referring to the accusations made against Armenians, Zohrab said, "They are all absolute slander. The local administration connived in the Adana Massacres. The first thug to attack was an administration official shouting, 'Long live Sultan Hamid.'[4]

By 1913, the Committee of Union and Progress, led by the triumvirate Talaat, Enver, and Jamal, had total control of the government. When the First World War began, Turkey aligned itself with Germany and Austria-Hungary. Turkish and Armenian men and boys were drafted into the Turkish army. My uncle, Minas (my father's eldest brother), and my father's uncle, Alexan, were both called up. My father's family was from the Armenian village of Keramet in the Southern Marmara region, close to Lake Iznik and the city of Bursa.

The extermination of the Armenians happened in well-planned stages. As the First World War progressed, Armenian soldiers fought alongside Turkish soldiers. But in the early spring of 1915, Armenian soldiers were disarmed and made to work in labor battalions. They were given little food and made to work until they died of starvation or exhaustion. Then, on April 24, 1915, two hundred and fifty Armenian leaders in important positions in Turkish society—whether civic, religious, cultural, or commercial—were arrested and transported by train to outlying regions of the empire and brutally killed. Eventually, the number of Armenian leaders arrested would be 2,345. Siamanto and Zohrab were in the initial group killed. Zabel Yessayan narrowly escaped, as she was alerted to what was happening and left Turkey.

The Armenians throughout the Ottoman Empire, thus, had no leaders to advocate for them or the Armenian soldiers to defend them. On May 27, 1915, the Ottoman parliament passed the Tehcir Law—in Turkish: Sevk ve Iskan Kanuna (translation: Deportation or Forced Displacement). Proclamations were posted in all areas with Armenian populations. The proclamation stated the following: 1) All Armenians except the sick are to leave their homes within five days under escort by armed guards; 2) Armenians are forbidden from selling their property or the lands they own; 3) Armenians are allowed to take only what they can carry; 4) Failure to cooperate meant Armenians would be forced to go or be killed. In Marash, those who complained or rebelled were hung immediately in full public view.

Procedures followed were basically the same everywhere. First, an army unit would visit a town or village. Weapons were collected and then those who avoided military service were arrested. Next, Armenian inhabitants were notified to be ready for deportation and told it was only a precautionary war measure—since Armenians were falsely accused of being traitors by the government in Istanbul—and that soon they would be allowed to return to their homes again. Armenians were promised they would be protected by the gendarmes who escorted them against attack by mobs or robbers. The reality was much different. The government let out of prison the worst sociopathic criminals who would then carry out the horrendous slaughter—first of the men and then any women, children, and elderly people still on the roads. These freed convicts were under the jurisdiction of the secret organization known as Teshkilati Makhsusiye. Before reaching the ultimate destinations of the wastelands of Syria and Mesopotamia, the prettier girls and women and children were taken by Turks, Kurds, or Arabs. The rest of the girls and women were subjected to mass rape and humiliation in every town or village through which they passed.

The Secretary of the Interior, Talaat Pasha, kept meticulous records of the missing and the dead in the six vilayets and other regions heavily populated by Armenians. Talaat's Black Book, with the statistics he compiled, can be accessed on the Internet.[5]

The young Turk leadership known as the Committee of Union and Progress succeeded in destroying Armenian life in Turkey which had lasted three millennia. Their ultimate objective was to remove all traces of Armenian life from Turkey. It was not enough for the Turkish leadership to exterminate, but it was also equally important for them to obliterate Armenian religious, cultural, and educational edifices. With this calculated destruction, the Turks transformed the landscape to conform to their political agenda. Turkey was to be a land for the Turks only and, according to the curriculum set in the 1930s under the leadership of Kemal Ataturk, it was the Turks who were there from the beginning of recorded history, not the Armenians or the Greeks.

After the catastrophic losses incurred by the Armenians during the Genocide of 1915-1923, there would be two more large scale killings of Armenians before the birth of the Turkish Republic in 1923. The

Battle of Marash 1920 would see the destruction of the Armenians of that city and neighboring cities, villages, and towns. This would be followed by the destruction of the city of Smyrna in 1922, where the Armenian neighborhood would be targeted first. People, as in the Genocide of 1915 and all subsequent massacres, were subjected to torture and death.

The Battle of Marash is the focus of this book. Miraculously, Armenians survived and upon leaving Turkey, many flourished, practiced their Christian faith without discrimination, started families, and began careers. All the while, they were ever mindful of those who never made it out alive. What follows is their story of survival.

CHAPTER 2
BATTLE OF MARASH, 1920

The Battle of Marash lasted three weeks in the early winter of 1920 from January 21 to February 13. It was a catastrophic, pointless disaster for the Armenians, the French, and the allies. The French forces were under the command of General Quérette and the Turkish National forces under the command of Mustafa Kemal Pasha.

The First World War ended for the Ottoman Empire when it surrendered to the allies in October of 1918. The victorious French and British were in competition for what lands remained of the Ottoman Empire. Each wanted to exert influence in Cilicia where Marash was located.

In February 1919, British troops came to Marash, bringing with them their military wagons and hundreds of Armenian deportees. By Saturday, March 8, 1919, Armenians who survived the deportations of the war years were encouraged to return to their homes in Cilicia. One hundred and fifty thousand Armenians returned. Of that number, 20,000 went back to Marash. Armenians felt confident enough with the British presence to resume normal activities.

Turks were forced to relinquish many of the homes and properties they had confiscated and occupied. A new era was dawning for the Armenians who had returned. They thought Turkey would be dismembered by the allies and Cilicia, which included Marash, would be given to the Armenians as mandated territory. The question was which of the allies: the British, French or the Americans would assume the mandate. The Armenian Catholics and the Gregorians favored a French mandate. The Protestants and a minority of the

Gregorians opted for an American mandate. Regardless of which power took charge, independence was in the air after 600 years of Turkish domination. Businesses were started and homes rebuilt and repaired with farms and vineyards cultivated once again.

The Turkish Christian Church opened with twelve members. Reverend Abraham Berberian was appointed pastor and the church was officially recognized as the Fourth Evangelical Church of Marash. In the same month of March, Near East personnel arrived, including Stanley Kerr and the Reverend James L. Lyman. The Americans took over the German hospital of Bettshallum.

In July of 1919, Mustafa Kemal drew up a national pact. A secret Kemalist army was created. A top Kurd and friend to Mustafa Kemal came to Marash. British officials were becoming very friendly with the Turkish officials of the city. Atah Bey openly began to distribute firearms and ammunition to the Turks of the city and surrounding villages. Once again, Armenians in the city and in nearby villages were robbed and killed.

Armenians who happened to be in close proximity to British soldiers heard rumors that the British would withdraw from Marash and Cilicia. The British government was under pressure to withdraw and demobilize. On September 15, 1919, Prime Minister David Lloyd George reluctantly accepted the proposal of Prime Minister George Clemenceau to have the French formally assume control of Cilicia. On Wednesday, October 29, 1919, French troops, with brave Armenian volunteers as a vanguard, victoriously entered Marash. Armenian leaders, including Professor Aram Toros Bagdikian, worked tirelessly to make sure either French or British soldiers were there so that the Armenians would not be subjected to reprisals by the Turks. On Saturday, November 1, the British withdrew.

While the French occupiers were promised much in material reinforcements by Field Marshall Ferdinand Foch, nothing arrived. French convoys and communication lines were regularly coming under attack by the Turkish forces. On January 17, General Quérette arrived in Marash from Adana.

On January 21, General Quérette summoned the Muslim notables to his headquarters, accused the Turkish forces of fermenting attacks, and told them to stop.

When the Turkish leaders left the meeting, the Turkish police chief, Arslan Toquz, took out his pistol and fired five rounds into the air. The Battle of Marash had begun. French soldiers and Armenian men, women, and children who were in the streets, unable to reach safe havens, were shot on the spot.

On that day, also, Armenians in surrounding villages were annihilated by the mob. Not a single Armenian would be spared. "Children were ripped open before their parents, their hearts taken out, and stuffed down their mothers' throats. Mothers were crucified naked to doors and, before their very eyes, their small ones were fixed to the floor with swords and left withering."[6]

Compounding the dire situation, there was no direct communication between the French and their division headquarters. General Dufieux in Adana only learned of the start of the Battle because Armenian legionnaires disguised themselves as Muslims and crossed battle lines.

There were seven safe military centers in Marash: 1) The Armenian girls' college; 2) The German Bett Shallum (Bettshallum) Orphanage; 3) The German hospital; 4) The Armenian Catholic Church; 5) The Latin monastery; 6) The Gregorian Church of Forty Children aka Karasoun Monoog; and 7) The First Armenian Evangelical Church—Reverend Hartunian's church. Almost half of the Armenians, about 10,000, managed to take refuge in these centers. The rest remained in their homes or in a number of unprotected church buildings.

On the night of January 23, in the middle of the conflagration with gunshots and cannons going off, the Turks began to set fire to Armenian houses and buildings, including churches where Armenian civilians had fled for safety. The Armenians unlucky enough to be in their homes in the Armenian and Turkish quarters were tortured and slaughtered. On Tuesday, January 27, the Church of the Holy Virgin with 2,500 Armenians who had gathered inside for safety was burned to the ground by the Turks. Kerosene had been brought in large cans. Cloth was soaked in the kerosene, ignited with fire, and thrown on the building.

As soon as Dufieux learned of the Battle, he appointed Lieutenant Colonel Robert Norman to lead a relief expedition. The relief consisted of three infantry battalions and half a squadron of cavalry. Aerial reconnaissance flights were dispatched giving hope to the French soldiers, Armenians, and American relief workers.

On February 7, Normand's unit fought its way into the city and began to bombard the Turkish positions with heavy artillery. Normand broke through Turkish lines to reach General Quérette's headquarters. On the same day, February 7, 1920, Karasoun Manoog church, with Armenian civilians inside burned to the ground, and 3,700 refugees were crammed into the Latin or Franciscan monastery on the hill. Then, Norman told Quérette something astonishing, which he claimed came from General Dufieux. The French would proceed with the full evacuation of the French garrison of Marash. All this occurred while the Turkish Nationalists were seeking a ceasefire. At 3:00 in the morning on February 11, Quérette destroyed the remaining ammunition dumps. He was even preparing to leave Marash in the dark in order to prevent the terrified Armenians from hindering the French withdrawal. However, the Armenians did learn of the French evacuation, and 3,000 Armenians managed to flee with the French in a three-day, seventy-five-mile long trek to Islahia. Mothers tied their infants and young children to their backs and only realized later that their children had frozen to death. But their deaths were merciful compared to the second group of Armenians who decided to follow the first group. They had taken shelter in the Catholic cathedral and attempted to follow the retreat. They were cut down by Turkish rifle and machine gun fire. Only a few—wounded, half dead and traumatized by what they went through—survived.

The Armenians who had followed the French walked hungry and thirsty through deep snow in the cold and wind. The old, the children, the weak, and the exhausted dropped and were left in the snow.

On February 14, 1920, the French, followed by the Armenians, reached Islahia. One third of those who started from Marash died on the way. Of those who reached Adana by train, many were taken to hospitals for medical attention and, in worst cases, had to have their feet or toes amputated; others went to Mersin, to Iskenderun, and some to Aleppo. Ten thousand Armenians remained in Marash at the cessation of the fighting. Near East officials and American missionaries gave them shelter, clothing, food, and provided them with work. This continued for two years.

In the Battle of Marash, 12,000 Armenian civilians died, along with 4,500 Turks, 1,200 French, and 150 Armenian legionnaires fighting with the French. By February of 1920, whatever churches and orphanages remained did so under severe restrictions.

Armenian survivors of the Battle of Marash were a symbol and reminder to the Turks and Kurds of the not-so-perfect genocide.

CHAPTER 3
LYDIA BAGDIKIAN

Let your light so shine before men,
that they may see your good works,
and glorify your Father which is in heaven.
—Matthew 5:16

Lydia Bagdikian (top left)

Lydia Bagdikian was the second eldest of four daughters and one son of Aram Toros Bagdikian and Dudeh ("Daisy") A. Uvezian Bagdikian. Lydia was raised in a loving Christian household in Marash, Turkey. Aram and Daisy were enlightened parents and came up with ingenious ways of raising their children. A memorable example of this was to give each child presents upon the birth of another child, letting each one know the gifts were on behalf of the new baby, thus, preventing jealousy.

Daisy always led by example and was without prejudice or ill feeling even toward people who did not harbor good intentions. She unobtrusively quoted from the scriptures when Lydia questioned injustices. Daisy's gentle manner and unselfish nature had a profound effect on her husband and children.

Aram, Lydia's father, was an admirable man who sacrificed going to America with his family, opting instead to stay on in Marash to help the beleaguered Armenians. He was a man of principal and, like Daisy, always chose the morally right position instead of the most expedient.

Lydia's family, like so many others, was caught up in the anti-Armenian frenzy of the young Turk government followed by similar behavior of the Kemalists. It was a very precarious time to be an Armenian.

During the First World War, Aram was a professor of chemistry and physics at the American St. Paul's College in Tarsus, which was 150 miles from Marash. The Bagdikian family would remain at the college compound until 1917 when the United States entered the First World War.

Lydia's family planned to leave Marash for the United States as soon as possible—but first they would visit Uncle Hagop, Daisy's brother in Aleppo, Syria. After seeing him, they would return to Marash to visit friends and say goodbye, after which Aram would sell his vineyards. Everything went according to plan when they returned to Marash for one last summer. What they saw in the city were survivors of the deportations of 1915-1916. This was a huge problem: all of these people needed help. Aram was elected to serve as chairman of the Armenian National Union, which represented all three Christian denominations, including that of the Apostolic church. Aram also accepted the position of superintendent of schools. He had to remind the committee that he would only hold both positions until a successor was chosen to replace him.

Once in Marash, the family moved back to their original home located near the American college, the American hospital, and Bethel, the school that at one time was a German-run orphanage for children who were survivors of previous wars and massacres.

One evening, as the committee of the Armenian National Union was conducting business, news reached them that the English army of occupation would be withdrawing from Marash and French troops would take over. The Armenians did not want to be at the mercy of the Turks again. Aram would be their spokesperson. He would speak on their behalf to the English general. Was the rumor true? He would have to meet with the British area commander in Adana to find out. No one wanted an interval of time between the British departure and the French arrival. A car was provided with an English driver to take Aram to Adana. On the way, the English driver and Aram were ambushed by Turkish guerilas. Luckily they both survived the gunfire unharmed. The British promised Aram that their soldiers would not leave Marash until the French arrived. Satisfied by the response, Aram returned to Marash.

French Army Troop C reached Marash on foot and horseback. Aram and a number of leading Armenian citizens of the city were there to thank and bid farewell to the departing English. Formal greetings were exchanged between the English and French, followed by Aram and members of the Citizens committee's introduction to the French.

Little did the Armenians know that events were conspiring that would change the lives of the Bagdikian family and everybody else, as another rumor was circulating that the French would be withdrawing from the city. The Turks heard the same rumor and were arming themselves for a massacre of the Armenians once the French left. The Armenians knew that time was running out and they needed to arm themselves. A scout was sent to find out about acquiring ammunition. When he returned, the plan was to send a dozen young, reliable men to get the weapons. But they needed a leader. Aram offered his help. Daisy, heavily pregnant, was upset but knew that many lives were at stake if her husband didn't go. He went and the expedition succeeded.

Fighting began on January 8, 1920, between the French and the Turks. Because the Bagdikians lived on the outskirts of Marash, every day scouts would bring the family news about what was happening in the city. Aram kept going back and forth between the Citizens committee and French headquarters. Daisy, awaiting the birth of her child, was now confined in the American hospital, which was on the road between the Bagdikian home and the road that led to Marash.

The rumors proved to be true. The French would leave. It was necessary to notify every single Armenian in Marash. The best way to do so was to get to the religious leaders. Couriers were sent out to notify them all. It was hoped the priests and ministers would gather their parishioners as quickly as possible. Those who wanted to follow the French could do so.

The Turks had compiled a list with the names of Armenian leaders to kill in the eventuality of a massacre. Aram Toros Bagdikian's name was on that list.

To throw the Turks off guard and to minimize the loss of life in case of hostilities, the French would leave in the middle of the night. The Bagdikian family got ready. Lydia was eleven, Tirzah was twelve, Cynthia was eight, and Nora was six years old. Aram was thirty-seven and Daisy was thirty-three years old. Even with a ten-day-old baby, Ben Hur, Daisy did not hesitate. They would follow the French. Daisy had already sewn valuable jewels into the clothing of her daughters. Lydia was given the family necklaces and bracelets to wear, in case they would have to sell them to survive. Their gold was too heavy to carry so they buried it and told their neighbors who remained where it was. Left behind were the oriental carpets, the family album, and household goods.

The French would take the most mountainous route away from the city. According to French military archives, on the night of the departure, the contingent consisted of 3,000 officers and men. Aram was even given a French uniform to disguise himself in case Turks were encountered along the way.

Suddenly, there was movement and the French began their withdrawal. French soldiers and the Armenians would be heading into a blizzard and one of the worst snowstorms in years.

On the outskirts of Marash, the Bagdikian family saw thousands of civilians mixed in with uniformed soldiers. Aram's relaying the enormity of the situation through couriers had reached all of the church leaders of the city.

As they began the withdrawal, Lydia recalled:

"It began to snow even harder. It was not only the white snow that made it seem almost daylight. I realized, shivering, that all eyes were looking toward the city. The city was on fire! 'That's the First Church burning!' someone cried. 'And the second church. And the Catholic Church. The third church. The Gregorian Church. The School House.' 'But they are full of people. The Christians went there to hide,' someone cried.

Now and then someone could be heard sobbing. All families had not left as a whole. Some fathers had left without the rest of the family. Some families had lost one another while escaping the city."[7]

CHAPTER 4
WALKING OR DYING

The following two chapters—"Walking or Dying" and "Islahia"—are taken in full from the book *The Memoir of Lydia Bagdikian,* edited by her brother Ben H. Bagdikian in 1997. Note that all items in {brackets} are Ellen Sarkisian Chesnut's clarifications. The following is a list of people and family members mentioned in these chapters:

- Aram Toros: Head of the family
- Dudeh "Daisy": Wife of Aram
- Cynthia: Lydia's sister, born January 8, 1911
- Nora: Lydia's sister, born on June 7, 1913
- Ben Hur: Lydia's brother, born on January 30, 1920
- Bedros: Male family servant
- Elmas: Female family servant
- Mozart: Family horse

"Walking or Dying" from *The Memoir of Lydia Bagdikian*:

The fourth day began with heavy hearts and new fears. We had found in the elements another enemy. We started out together and remained together a little longer than usual. The fact that there had been a few skirmishes with same chetahs {non-official members of the Turkish army, thought of as brigands} the night before did not concern people so much as what we had begun to see today—more people stopping to bury their dead. Once in a while we would see a body no one claimed maybe because no one in his family knew he had stopped his flight. I don't remember being shocked at anything that day. I remember I felt my feet aching. I tried to imagine a snow pile was a rock on which I could sit but Tirzah was right with me and she would not let me stop. I began to cry.

"Once you stop it will be harder to start again," she pleaded with me. She kept close by my side. Mother and Cynthia were walking today. Papa was leading Mozart with only blankets for a load.

"Why is Mother walking?" I asked Tirzah.

"Everyone has to walk today. People who don't walk will freeze to death."

I felt ill and tired and sleepy.

"These people were walking but they died just the same," I cried, looking at the dead bodies around which we had to walk. Such a sight was getting to be more common as the day wore on.

A woman's hysterical cries aroused me from my apathy.

"My boy, my boy," she was crying upon discovering the body of her child. She had lost him in today's blizzard. Some said it was snowing again, others said it was just the wind.

"God," another woman cried, seeing the face of the distraught mother.

I wanted to say, "I hate God," but I was afraid. I thought He would hear me and maybe freeze someone in our family. Sometimes, in fact most of the time, I could not understand God. I was even more confused when I heard the conversation of two women who were walking very near to me.

"This death," one was saying to the other, "is much easier than dying of thirst as I almost did on the road to Der-El-Zor. The heat is much worse than cold."

I had not been warm for so long that it was hard for me to agree with her, although I was not included in the conversation. No one even noticed that I was listening or understanding. I was just trudging along, still trying to understand God's ways. I wondered if He could see how miserable we all were and why He was not doing something about it. I decided as soon as I had a chance I would ask

Mother about it. I knew she would have the right answer but I could not imagine what the answer would be.

The ladies were still talking.

"At least snow purifies the air. There are more sicknesses during extreme heat when unsanitary conditions exist," seemed to be the gist of their conversation.

"We prayed for just a breeze," she continued. "And do you know how it feels to be thirsty? And no one whips us here when we stop. No wild Turks here to attack young girls. I remember the day the wild Turkish guides stripped us and made us march naked in the hot sun…"

Tirzah had been listening too. Now she pushed me forward.

"Let us run and we'll almost be with Mother," she said. But I was still thinking about what the ladies had said and again I wondered why God had not struck those guards dead.

"That God!" I said.

"What did you say?" Tirzah asked.

"I don't care what God thinks," I said. "I don't care if He makes me freeze. I am sleepy and I am going to lie down and sleep for a few minutes."

Tirzah took hold of me and pushed me forward. We came up to Elmas with Ben Hur. She looked dejected, too, but, as usual, did not say anything.

When we caught up with Mother I was ready to break down and, but before I had a chance to give vent to my feelings, I saw her face. She looked ill. Papa looked worried too.

"Are you all right?" he asked us and then tried to persuade Mother to ride on Mozart again.

"Just for a while," he said. "You've got to keep moving."

Cynthia had not done much walking so far but Papa said she must walk for the rest of the day for her own good.

Mozart seemed happy to have Mother back on him, I thought. He could always tell when someone else rode him.

"Remarkable that he has not lost a shoe," Papa said. Papa could always find something to say. Whenever we had guests Papa did most of the talking. He never was without a story or a subject. I had never thought of Mozart's shoes. I looked down at my own shoes. They had burst open!

"My shoes," I cried, but no one heard me so I kept trudging on.

"I think we are going to stop soon," Papa said. "The line ahead is slowing down."

This was good news to me. It had been a long day, even longer than all the other days. I felt sick. That's the last I remembered of that day.

When I woke up, it was dark. People were either sleeping, sitting or stretched out on the white ground. Now and then one could hear someone sobbing or a baby crying. Always there would be someone crying. I did not know where we were or what time it as but I tried to see if we were all there. We were always losing Nora and Bedros but tonight they had caught up with us.

It was getting light enough so I could make out the familiar faces. Sometimes I dreaded daylight because it meant more walking and I was getting so tired and each day seemed colder than day before.

I never remembered being hungry but I remembered being very sleepy. I liked being sleepy because then I did not feel the cold so much. I dreamed of my warm bed and wondered if someday I would be in a warm bed again. I wondered if it would be possible to forget this cold and this nightmare. I wanted to think and think so the time would pass. Somehow the time would pass and we would start a new day.

We always prayed before we started. Every family had someone with a Bible. I hoped God would see all these people with their Bibles and think they were good so He would do something to make them happy and reward them for trusting in Him. Papa had brought a small pocket Bible. But Mother's favorite Bible, with our dates of birth, names, important events in the life of our family, was buried with the gold left behind.

In later years when we wondered who had taken our gold, I often wondered how people would feel stealing something when they knew to whom it belonged. The Bible would be with it. A few neighbors had known about it when Papa buried it all.

Before we started, Mother reminded us of the zwieback in our pockets and asked how much we had left. Just then some kind man brought us milk. Mother seemed surprised. A few men had rounded out a few stray cows during the night. "That's a good sign," someone said.

Before I had a chance to feel hopeful, someone added, "It could be a bad sign. Where did the cows come from? Are we near a Turkish village? Or maybe Armenians from a nearby village are being driven out."

I felt at ease, however, when Papa said by tomorrow we would reach Islahia where we could probably take a train. The army would get there first and take over the railway station. It was not being run by Turks. The army of occupation still controlled that section.

I always tried to believe what I wanted to believe. I never remembered thinking so much before. My head was full of thoughts that I never had before. Just walking had become such a habit that I would walk for miles and then suddenly stop to see where I was, who I was.

I realized suddenly that I was being pushed around. We had come to a narrow passage. I could see the sky when I looked up but on both sides the snow was so high it seemed I was going through a white tunnel. I could not see anyone familiar. Instinctively I tried to run but could not. I was stepping on people lying on the ground. I was horrified.

"Excuse me," I said.

"Little girl, don't waste your breath saying 'Excuse me,'" a woman in back said. "They can't hear you. They are dead!"

Ordinarily, I would have been frightened. But I seemed to be in a stupor. I didn't say "Excuse me" anymore. I tried to walk around or over the bodies. When the tunnel began to get wider and the snow had blown away from the bodies on the ground, I could see that the bodies were those of the Algerian soldiers. Some were blacker than others, I thought. People had taken their coats.

"They'll be cold," I said, thinking out loud.

"They're the only ones who are not cold now," I heard that same woman say

I wondered why she was following me. I wanted to get away from her.

Then I realized she had answered my thoughts in Turkish. She must understand English, I thought. I was so sure I had really thought this in silence when she answered, "You must be one of the Bagdikians."

I nodded in silence and tried to forge my way ahead. It was too cold to open my mouth.

Now I saw before me a whole row of dead men—naked! Every bit of clothing had been taken away from them.

"To keep the live ones warm," the voice in back said.

"I didn't say a word," I thought, "and she could not see my face."

Then I stumbled and fell on one of the dead bodies. I didn't dare cry or appear frightened. I didn't want the lady following me to say anything else.

I wondered if God saw all these dead people and if He saw me fall on one. While I was thinking, I almost tripped again but the woman in back caught me.

"You won't hurt them by walking on them," she said. "They're dead, They're lucky."

Now I really wanted to run away.

"Tirzah!" I called.

I heard her answer. I had not realized she was just ahead of me. I could walk a little faster now. The dead bodies were farther apart. I caught up with Tirzah and Elmas who was cuddling Ben Hur. I stopped.

"I want to lie down for a few minutes," I said.

"You mustn't!" Tirzah said.

"But I'm so sleepy."

"You mustn't!" Tirzah scolded me.

"I'm too sleepy to walk." I was crying. "Let me sleep just for a few minutes."

"No!" Tirzah said more insistently.

I bargained with her.

"Let me lie down just for a few seconds," I pleaded. "Up to twenty. Count up to twenty. I'll get up then," I promised.

"No!" she shouted.

"The poor girl, let her lie down for a few minutes," Elmas said.

Tirzah whispered something in her ear. Then both of them tried to drag me. I bargained again.

"Count to only ten," I pleaded. "If you'll just let me close my eyes for a few minutes, I promise I won't stop again."

Now they both shouted, "No! You must not stop!"

I began to cry.

"Count to five,' I said. I was so sleepy. If all the wealth in the world had been offered to me, I would not have exchanged it for a few seconds of sleep. "I'm too sleepy to go any farther," I said, and fell to the ground. Tirzah pulled me up, slapped my face and shook me.

"I have to. I have to." Now Tirzah began to cry.

"You're a Turk, that's what you are!" I yelled. "How can you be so cruel at a time like this? You're a Turk, that's what you are." I was crying, too.

"I have to! I have to!" Tirzah was sobbing.

I heard the woman near me say "Once they go to sleep, that's the end. If you go to sleep now, you'll be like the soldiers on the ground."

"Well, don't let anyone take my clothes!" I said.

"If you go to sleep, they will," she said.

"Well, I won't let them," I said, and started to walk again, angry.

It must have been a relief to Tirzah and Elmas to arouse enough anger in me to make me walk again. I didn't realize it at the time that Tirzah had saved my life.

As soon as Tirzah felt it safe to let me alone for a while, she started to run ahead calling for Papa. Soon we saw him walking towards us. Tirzah ran ahead to meet him.

"She is telling him about me," I thought.

"If you weren't such a big girl, I would carry you," Papa said. "But don't forget you were eleven last month. And you must walk for your own safety. Tomorrow the walking will be over and we'll be in a warm place again." "I am dreaming," I thought and followed him. We stopped just for a second to look inside Ben Hur's bundle. Papa dug into some clean snow and put it in his mouth.

"Ice cream for the baby," he said. Yes, he was still breathing. He was nine days old when we left. This was our sixth day. He must have been two weeks old.

[A short time before his death in 1957, my father told me that he had, in fact, believed that I had frozen to death, but kept it a secret for fear that it would demoralize the rest of the family. When my mother began to faint and fall off her horse, my father dropped his supposedly frozen bundle and when "the bundle" hit the ground, I cried. BHB {recollection by Ben H. Bagdikian}]

We were now in an open plain. People seemed to be scattered. There were a few here and a few there, not in bunches as there had been earlier in the day. Now we were seeing bodies of little children on the ground. People would stop to see if they were their children. Once in a while we could see someone take a scarf or coat from a dead person.

"How can they?" I thought.

I wouldn't wear something belonging to a dead person.

At first, I wanted to go by the dead bodies as fast as I could. But soon I found myself throwing sidelong glances— just to make sure it was not one of the family. What a horrid thought! Then I would start to run. Soon we caught up with Mother and Cynthia. We were all together now except Nora and Bedros. "Why can't he keep up with us?" Mother sighed.

"After all, she is a heavy bundle to carry," Papa said.

"I should realize that," Mother said. "She is six years old. Almost seven-in June.

June seemed so far away. It was the middle of February now.

"I wonder where we will be in June," I thought. "Even if we don't have a bed by then, at least it will be warm."

Up to now I had not given much thought to the seasons. It seemed I had lived a lifetime in one week. I could remember days of fear during the war when we wondered if we would be the next to be exiled. I remembered the fear in Mother's eyes when she knew we were in court the day the gendarme had driven us from our summer home to the city. I remembered so well her terrified face when Papa was brought home, unconscious, in a stretcher. Yes, we had known fear, but never deprivation. Now we knew fear, discomfort, pain. Now I ached all over. My toes were sticking out of my shoes. The shoes had burst open.

It was soon dusk. Far ahead on the horizon we could see a few objects that looked like sheds or stables. As we approached it and dusk turned into darkness, we saw a light ahead.

People were saying, "Could that be the station? Islahia?"

Someone was coming towards us. He stopped to talk with Papa. We gathered around him. Papa was talking to him in Turkish. Soon the people behind us caught up with us. Some were talking in Turkish, some in Armenian. Whenever Turkish was spoken, I could understand.

"You can reach Islahia in a few more hours," the man was saying, "but it will be safer to stop here tonight and rest. Too many have died today. There will be some sort of shelter. We seem to be in a deserted village. We have caught a few stray cows. The men are killing the cows now so we can all have meat. If they can milk them before they kill them, there might be milk for the babies. There is a little wood in some of the huts. You're within reach of help and safety. I advise you to be patient and stay here at night."

"If this is a deserted village, the enemy must be near," someone said. I'm not going to take a chance and stop. I'm going ahead."

Some agreed with him and went ahead.

"What do you think?" Papa asked Mother.

"Let's stay," Mother said.

Papa seemed relieved. "Tirzah and Lydia are too tired. I think it best for us all to stay."

We stayed in a large, empty room, with no floors.

"Is this a stable?" I asked Mother

"It's too clean for a stable," Mother said. "People must have lived here.

"But there is no furniture," I said.

"Probably they took everything with them," Mother replied.

Soon the men had found firewood and built a fire. It was heavenly to be warm again. Then there was sizzling meat. How good it smelled! People were devouring it.

"My kingdom for some salt," someone said.

People were actually laughing!

"Would anyone think of bringing salt from Marash?" someone said, jokingly. There was more laughter.

"Thank God for food even without salt," Papa laughed.

I noticed he was going in and out of the hut. Each time he returned, Mother would give him an anxious look. We knew what it was. Again, we were all here except Nora.

"I hope he'll at least stop here to look for us," Mother said.

Papa wanted to reassure her.

"If he does not," he said, "maybe he'll have reached Islahia by the time we get there tomorrow."

"But he is always behind us," Mother reminded him.

"I know," Papa said, "but when he finds out he is so near the end of the journey, he might hurry."

There were others looking for dear ones. People were stopping at the different huts, asking if so-and-so was there. Papa went to look in all the huts but came back without news. Now he was utterly dejected.

"God has been with us all through this journey," Mother said. "Let's not doubt Him now." Each was trying to reassure the other.

We children sat in silence, our parents' faces and words the barometers for us to watch.

Ben Hur was sleeping peacefully. Papa had read somewhere that the name Ben Hur meant "Child of Fire." Here was the "Child of Fire," two weeks old, fed on melting snow. He had escaped from a burning city through snow and ice. What fate was in store for him.

With anxious hearts, we fell asleep, using one another's laps for pillows. Too soon we were reminded that it was still cold because the wood fire soon turned to ashes.

During my drowsy moments I imagined this but to be the manger in which Jesus was born. I had seen pictures of it in Sunday School. That manger was much smaller than this, though. Thinking of Jesus made me think that surely He would watch over Nora. I needed Him so desperately tonight that I promised I would not doubt His goodness again. We were almost at the end of our journey. Surely, He would not spoil all this by having something awful happen to Nora! Not even to punish me for the unkind thoughts I had about Him sometimes.

"In that case He should punish me," I thought. But secretly I thought that's not always how He works! Then I caught myself doubting Him again.

"I mustn't!" I thought. "I mustn't."

I really wanted Him to know I wanted to trust Him. Every waking moment I was praying for Nora's safety. Papa had prayed that night, as he had every night. Almost everyone prayed every night. Often on the road the old ladies would pray all day long.

"Why did He hear some of the prayers and not others?" I thought. Then I was frightened because I was afraid it might seem like doubting Him again. I really wanted to trust Him. I found myself bargaining with Him—"If you'll protect Nora and let us all reach safety, I'll never mistrust You again," I had prayed.

"Everybody is praying. Can He hear everyone?" I thought, the more I thought, the more puzzled I became.

Often I had thought how difficult it must be to be parents. They had to think of everything. Tonight, especially, it seemed good to be a child.

I could not help thinking of Nora but I trusted Mother and Papa to find her. I felt I could go to sleep. There was Mother and Papa to find Nora.

"Is it all right to go to sleep?" I asked Mother.

"Of course, darling," she said, her eyes following my feet. It was beginning to hurt again but I did not want to complain. Mother had Nora to think about. She always seemed to know what we were thinking about.

"We can all go to sleep," she said. "Our Heavenly Father has taken care of us so far. He will not forsake us now."

Just then the thought came to me that, Mother and Papa, too, had someone to worry for them. God looked after them the way they looked after us. As I began to get drowsier and drowsier, I thought maybe that's what was meant by "children of God."

I dreamed all night but I could not remember clearly any of the dreams. When I woke up Papa was not with us. We had fallen into the habit of counting everyone before going to sleep and as soon as awakening.

"Where is Papa?" we all seemed to ask simultaneously.

"He went to see if he could find Nora and Bedros," Mother said.

As she prepared us for the final lap of our walking, Papa walked in. We knew he had not found Nora.

"They must have continued to Islahia," he said, trying to be reassuring. "We will wait for them there if they are not already there."

CHAPTER 5

ISLAHIA

"Islahia" from *The Memoir of Lydia Bagdikian*:

It was morning again. I had been awakened because my pillow was moving. I don't know on whose lap I had been resting my head. People were getting ready to go. It was easy to start out again. We had not undressed for six nights so there was no dressing to do.

I realized again with a start that Nora was not with us. I reminded God of my promise.

We said our morning prayers and started out again, always looking ahead to see if Nora and Bedros were ahead of us. Sometimes we looked behind. If she had not reached the village during the night, she must either be ahead or there was little hope of seeing her. We all seemed to sense this without putting it into words.

Mother could hardly talk. She had a very bad cold. I did not feel cold anymore. I felt feverish. Mother noticed when I took off my scarf.

"Don't," she said, "even if you feel hot. You still need its protection. We'll soon be there."

She looked at my feet. My toes were peeping through the burst shoes. The toes were swollen. The thoughts of Nora had made me forget my feet.

With heavy hearts we started out again. Before very long we were horrified to find so many dead bodies on the ground. The nearer we approached Islahia, where Papa said we would reach a railroad station, the more dead people we saw. Anxious ones were stopping to see the dead faces. Could one of them be a loved one? When I saw Papa looking too, I was frightened.

Maybe he is looking for Nora, I thought, horrified. I could see Mother and Cynthia ahead on Mozart. Papa would lead them for a while and walk back to see if Tirzah and I and Ben Hur and Elmas were all right. Of course, he was also always looking for Nora and Bedros whether he was going forward or coming back to check on us.

"Going, coming back, and going again," Tirzah said, "makes him walk twice more than the rest of us!"

I had not thought of this. Tirzah could do arithmetic much better than I. This observation of hers occupied me a few minutes. I was always glad to think about something so the time would pass. Going over dead bodies seemed so natural by now. Most of them were still Algerian soldiers. At first the nude bodies had shocked me but now I had seen so many that I would never be shocked again.

In six days I had grown six years. I had learned to think. What else was there to do? I either had to think to pass the time or I wanted to lie down and go to sleep. But Tirzah had never let me alone. If I slowed down, she would slow down. If I ran ahead, she could watch me.

The morning of the sixth day was a clear day. It had stopped snowing. In some spots the drift had raised the snow so high that one could not see ahead. I soon realized that I was out in an open space now and could see several men on horseback coming towards us. I thought I was imagining things but the men and the horses were real. They were throwing bread right and left to the hungry, cold men and women. I didn't feel hungry so I did not pick up anything. But I tried to walk faster to keep up with Mozart.

Papa, Mother and Cynthia had stopped for a few minutes so we could catch up with them. Papa had picked up bread—I think it was zwieback again—and gave us all a piece. I knew, however, that he and Mother were looking back for hopes of seeing Nora but there was no one within eye's distance who looked like Nora or Bedros.

"Let us go on," Papa said to Mother. "Maybe they are already there. Look! There is the railroad station! We are almost in Islahia!"

By this time, we were all together except Nora and Bedros. With heavy hearts we started on the last lap of our journey. Yes, we had reached the railroad station. Several of the officers we knew from Marash were there rounding up the soldiers who had survived. In this struggle for survival over the elements, age had made no difference. Young and old alike succumbed, maybe the old because of frailty and maybe the young because of lack of the will to live. Who knows?

An officer beckoned to Papa. He took him aside to talk with him. He came back with the news.

The only train today will leave in a few minutes. It will take only the French soldiers," he had told Papa. However, he had added, "You have been of great help to us in keeping up the morale of your people and I think I can arrange to have your family go on this train to Adana. No other civilians will be allowed."

We should have been overjoyed but each felt the heart and thoughts of the others. We could not go without Nora.

The soldiers were filling up the train. Not even all of them could get on this train. One of the officers came to help Mother and us on the train. "You are ill, Madame," he said in French and we want to help you. He had been to our house many times to dinner. He had not forgotten us now.

"Thank you, but I cannot go without Nora," Mother said without hesitation. The officer knew Nora well. No one who came to the house could forget her.

"But she can come on the next train," he said, half-heartedly.

By this time many people had gathered around us. Some were kind, many were unkind.

"You are lucky to be so privileged," one bitter woman said to Mother. "What I would give to get on that train."

"I wish they would take you in my place," Mother said. "But I cannot leave unless all my children are with me."

"You should be thankful that you have lost only one," I heard someone else say, "God has been kinder to you than to me. I lost my two children I saw them freeze. I could not make a grave for them."

Mother began to weep.

"God comfort you," she said, "but I did not see my child

die. She may be living and I cannot leave here without knowing what happened to her.

"You had a servant look after her," someone else said bitterly.

The train whistle blew. The officer came again.

"Madame, you must decide," he said with authority, though trying to be kind. "The train will leave in a few minutes."

"Bedros!" Papa shouted just then.

We turned around, our hearts sinking. Yes, it was Bedros but Nora was not with him.

"Where is she? Where is she?" we all shouted.

"I don't know," he said. "When we left this morning she said she wanted to walk."

"But why did you not at least hold her hand?" Papa said. "How could you be so unreliable? You gave me your word of honor that you would not desert her and I gave you my word of honor that I would reward you generously."

At this, Bedros' face sank. The reward? He needed it now. He would be in a strange city. He had never left Marash before.

The officer came again.

"Madame," he said, "my superior officer has been most kind and patient and is willing to wait, but he, too, has orders."

"I cannot leave," Mother said.

We children said nothing. Mother was always right.

The officer turned to Papa.

"You have other children and your sick wife to think about," he said, trying to persuade Papa.

I could not understand everything, but a word here and a word there and with what others surrounding us were repeating, we knew what was going on.

"I don't blame her," one mother said.

"She should think of the other children," another said. "Look at that one with her frozen toes sticking out," she said, pointing to me. "She will be in the hospital many months."

"I won't go unless my mother does!" I cried.

It was a tense moment. Only the neighing of Mozart aroused us. Then Mother almost fainted.

"Nora's green scarf!" she cried.

Mother called to a woman who was passing us, one of the stragglers still coming toward the station.

"My daughter's scarf!" Mother cried.

"It's mine," the woman said.

"Let me look at it," Mother pleaded. "I don't think there was another like it in Marash."

Mother looked closely

"It is my daughter's," Mother cried. "I won't take it from you. Just tell me the truth. Where did you find it?"

"It was on the ground and I was cold," the woman admitted. "Surely you cannot blame me."

Now the woman was crying.

"You may have it," Mother said, "but please tell me, just where did you find it? Was it today, near here? Or where?"

The train blew its whistle and jolted. Now a larger crowd had gathered around us.

"Oh, dear God," Mother was praying, "help me do the right thing. I have my other children, my baby, my husband with me, but how can I leave, not knowing where Nora is, if she is living or dead?"

"Take that train, take that train," a hysterical woman was shouting. "What I would give to have at least one of my children and my husband here and the chance to ride on that train!"

"Take some of the sick people in our place," Mother pleaded with the officer.

"The permission is for your family only," he said. "I am sorry."

It seemed like eternity since we had arrived in Islahia. I found later it had not been more than an hour. But that hour stands more vividly in my mind than the six days and six nights. On those days and nights there was no decision to be made. We just stopped when the soldiers stopped. We started when the soldiers started. We had a destination. Now, in this darkest of all the hours, we had no destination. How terrible it was not to have a destination! How terrible it was not to know where a dear one was!

In the past at times like this I used to think, "What about tomorrow? By tomorrow, we will know what happened today." But sometimes we dreaded what could happen tomorrow. But

I did not have to make the decision. I was a child. I had a father and a mother to make the decision.

God was good to children who had a father and a mother. Just then I thought of the children who had come through without their fathers and their mothers. I was horrified. I wanted to make sure Mother and Papa were there. Yes, there they were. But they did not know when to begin to mourn, when to give up hope.

The train whistle blew again. It seemed louder this time. And the black smoke from the locomotive seemed to reach the skies. The locomotive was going in small motions back and forth, as if practicing for a race.

"I hope something is wrong with it," I thought, "so they can't go until Nora comes, if Nora comes..."

Mozart's neighing aroused us all.

"Nora!" Mother shouted. "My Nora! That's her. No one else walks like that."

"The poor woman is losing her mind," someone said. She has begun to imagine things."

But everyone was following Mother's eyes. Yes! It was Nora, trudging through the snow leisurely—a lone figure. She must have been several hundred yards away. She was just like a speck in the bright sun against the white snow, but you could tell it was Nora.

[From other family members, the arrival of Nora was even more dramatic because she was almost naked. BHB {recollection by Ben H. Bagdikian}]

When we shouted, she began to cry and run. Papa ran towards her. He picked her up in his arms. It was a miraculous reunion. When she reached us with Papa, we all began to cry with joy.

"God must have singled you out," cried the bitter woman who had lost her dear ones, with envy, I am sure, but no jealousy in her heart. I am sure she must have known that sadness and tragedy befalling others could not bring her dear ones back.

The puffing of the locomotive and another whistle from the train made us realize that it had not left yet. Mother and Papa were trying to gather us together. Our friend, the French officer, had heard the excitement and was there to help us children on the train. A neigh from Mozart made us realize that he was with us, too.

Just then Bedros appeared, appealing to Papa for help. In his joy, Papa could do nothing but forgive him.

*   *   *

The snapshot above, probably taken in 1922 in the Boston area, shows the author of the previous memoir chapters ("Walking or Dying" and "Islahia"). Lydia Natalie Bagdikian, then 13 years old, far left in the back row. Also shown are other members of her family who figure in the memoir. Next to Lydia are her father, Aram Bagdikian, then 40 years old, and Tirzah, then 15 years old. In the front row are Cynthia on the left, then 11 years old, and Nora on right, then 9 years old. Missing is a major family member, her mother, who was hospitalized, and Ben Hur, then 2 years old, presumably being cared for at home by a family friend.

*   *   *

Many years later, noted journalist Ben H. Bagdikian learned of the memoir written by his sister, Lydia. It chronicled her childhood in Turkey and in America as a young immigrant. Lydia died at the age of eighty-four in 1993, seventy years after the death of her beloved mother Daisy Uzevian Bagdikian on July 5, 1923. Lydia was buried in the same cemetery plot as her mother at Mt. Hope Cemetery in Boston, Massachusetts.

From the "Editor's Note" of *The Memoir of Lydia Bagdikian*:

"When Lydia died in Wakefield, Massachusetts in 1993, as her executor, I found among her effects the collected pages of her memoir. The memoir consisted of 417 typed pages in two loose-lead binders. A meticulous typist, she clearly had written it in her apartment in whatever time she could spare while holding a responsible and demanding position in the office of the Superintendent of Schools of Stoneham, Massachusetts. Most of the pages were typed double-spaced on one side of the paper, but some were single-spaced on both sides, and many had lines and phrases added in pencil, hinting of her need to make changes hurriedly in brief moments of free time. In the margins of some pages are red-penciled notes in Gregg shorthand, in which she was skilled. Not knowing Gregg or her intentions for them, I have made no attempt to translate the Gregg notations in this reproduction of her memoir.

The memoir printed here is as Lydia wrote it. I have made no changes with the exception of minor transpositions of words clearly typed by her in haste. I have also inserted occasional editorial clarifications of context in order to make a reference by Lydia more clear for younger generations who may be unfamiliar with the particular history of the time and circumstances.

Lydia's memoir...ends with the family finally reaching safety within the United States only to be devastated by the loss of our much-loved mother.

The memoir ends with the death of our mother, Daisy Uvezian Bagdikian, on July 5, 1923, when my mother was 36, and Lydia was 14 years old.

Ben H. Bagdikian,
Berkeley, California, USA
December 13, 1997"

CHAPTER 6
INTRODUCTION TO
DICRAN BERBERIAN:
A BIOGRAPHY BY RAFFI BERBERIAN

The following excerpt is from the biography, *A Remembrance of My Parents: Dicran and Armine Berberian*, written by Dicran Berberian's son, Raffi Berberian, in 1988:

My parents' origins are in Cilicia, that region of Eastern Turkey where a-large community of Armenians had lived for centuries under Ottoman rule. Both sides of my family had come under the influence of missionaries to Asia Minor from Europe and America, most notably Congregationalists from New England. My father's father, Abraham, was a product of the schools, colleges and seminary of the Armenian Evangelical community. As a young husband, he had faced tragedy, losing his wife and, a year later, their first child, to typhoid fever. His family name, Aghchigian, meaning the "son of a maiden" was hardly considered appropriate for a professor or clergyman, and so, while a seminary student, he took the name of Berberian, meaning the "son of a barber" which was in fact his status in life. In photographs, my grandfather's stern and distinguished appearance confirms the image of a Puritanical intellectual, emphatically engendering respect in the coat-and-tie uniform of a Congregationalist cleric. He was known for his brilliance in scholastic subjects and, specifically, for his superb command of the Turkish language and its calligraphy, which he taught in several institutions, the American Academy for Boys in

Marash, the United Central School (Miatzial Getronagan Varjaran) and ultimately in the school of the Beitshalom Orphanage operated by German Missionaries of the Deutsche Hilfsbund. Abraham Khodja (teacher) Berberian's temperament, I am told, was better suited to theological pursuits than to pastoral activities. Fortunately, his fits of choler found the ideal antidote in the woman he chose to be his second wife, Shamiram Nalbandian, a native of the town of Kilis and a graduate of the Girl's Seminary of Aintab, whom he married in 1902. Shamiram "Khanum" (Khanum being a Turkish title of respect for a married woman of social position) was known as a lady of sweetness, dignity and gentility. Her family was also Protestant, and her brother-in-law, Hagop Agha Shamlian, was the most successful tanner of hides in the City of Marash, where my grandparents settled shortly after the birth of my father, Dicran, in the City of Diarbekir in 1903.

Marash is nestled in the foothills of the Taurus Mountains. Like Rome, it was built upon seven hills. The magnificent stone lion created by the Hittites some 3,000 years ago still stands at the gate of the Citadel, the city's ancient landmark. The municipal water supply and sewage systems were remarkably advanced. Abundant water from mountain springs was fed to the city through clay pipes. Waste water was then channeled to the Kanli Dere, the "Bloody Valley," a stream which runs through the center of the city and eventually into the Ak-Sou River which empties into the Mediterranean Sea. Marash had become a prosperous and forward moving commercial center. Until about the turn of the century, its diverse ethnic groups had lived peacefully for centuries, but over this city, remote in the Turkish interior, loomed the specter of the decaying Ottoman Empire (known as the Sick Man of Europe) which governed the region. The allure of world politics and nascent yearnings for national self-determination became apparent among the Armenians of this distant outpost.

Today in America, the role of orphanages is relatively minor, but in Turkey at the turn of the century, these institutions became increasingly common in cities like Marash and, indeed, essential, for the massacres of Armenians which had taken place in 1895 and 1909 had left a surfeit of homeless children. Concerned individuals in the West (as well as the Orthodox Church in Russia) had responded to this need by raising funds to establish and maintain orphanages to care for the innocent children, where they would receive an education and learn a trade. Often the handicrafts created by the orphans were sold abroad to bring in additional income. In response to the accelerated persecution of the Christians, the missionaries directed their efforts increasingly to the Armenians. My paternal grandmother, Shamiram Khanum, assumed the role of matron consecutively in several orphanage asylums, in which capacity she served nobly, so that during various periods, the family boarded in these hostels, and, my father, though not yet an orphan himself, lived among children who had no material goods and who had suffered the greatest of childhood's hardships in having lost their parents. These were harrowing times, yet waves of persecution were interrupted by periods of relative tolerance during which the Armenian community prospered through hard work and industry. My grandfather bought a house in 1914, but put off moving in until five years later, finding it safer to keep himself and his family in the protection of orphanages and missions operated by foreigners. Turkey had entered the First World War on the side of Germany, while America was yet neutral. Thus, British charitable institutions were turned over to the Americans, and Armenians looked to the German missionaries for protection. Shortly after the defeat of Germany and the Armistice, the British Expeditionary Forces entered Marash, and this time the Americans assumed control of formerly German institutions.

In 1888, my mother's father, Vartan Poladian, married Leah Sarkissian, the daughter of a Presbyterian minister, who with his wife and other children had resettled to Connecticut in earlier waves of immigration. (During the time of the Civil War {mid-1880s}, her father, the Reverend Sarkissian had completed his theological studies at the Yale Divinity School. Her maiden aunts, Rachel and Hosanna, had become nurses. For a time, Aunt Rachel nursed in the clinic of the nationally distinguished New Haven pediatrician, Dr. Arnold Gesell.) Vartan Poladian also had had the chance to begin a new life in the safety of the United States, having come to New York University where he did graduate work in medicine. But obedient to the duty to serve his own people, he returned to Marash, where he was one of four medical doctors in this city of about 65,000 people, of which 30,000 were Armenians. There were few exclusively Turkish or Armenian ghettos in the city proper, but, within the bounds of the Township, a number of villages, including Zeitoun, Fundejak and Derekeoy, were inhabited almost exclusively by Armenians, bringing the total Armenian population of the area to nearly 86,000. The 1915 wave of deportations initially was directed toward these neighboring communities, and the inhabitants of Marash were witness to the successive trains of refugees wending their way through the city to almost certain death in the desert.

Dr. Poladian also was known as a stern man, though I am told that with his patients he had the gentle manner of a benevolent family physician. His wife was a lady of taste, beauty, refinement and saintly disposition, celebrated for the extraordinary hospitality of her home on the hillside of the Sheikh Mahallesi quarter of the city. She made it her mission in life to minister to the less fortunate. Witnessing the pitiful misery of Armenians under deportation passing through town, she did whatever she could to ease their suffering. Dr. Poladian was respected by many, not only because of his professional rank (he was Municipal Doctor of the City), but for his wisdom. He counseled the Armenian Community to try to be good citizens of the Empire, to refrain from forming entanglements with potentially unreliable foreign "Christian" powers and to stop making dangerous provocations against the Turkish government. But from the extremist elements who belonged to the Armenian political parties, his pleas for caution brought him ridicule and even threats against his life. No doubt this familial heritage is the source of the fear and respect which my parents accord to governmental authority, and from this painful history are derived their reluctance to become affiliated with partisan politics of any ilk and their repugnance for nationalism by any people.

So it was that both sets of grandparents, as notable members of the Evangelical community in Marash came into frequent contact with Western missionaries, as doctor, teacher, matron and social companion. Their position in society and their association with the Germans, the British and the Americans and with prominent and kindly Turkish friends saved them from deportation.

After World War I, Armenians had been led to believe that the Ottoman Empire would be dismembered by the Allies through the establishment of mandated territories. (In fact, during the War, the Allies had given to the Armenians assurances that, in the event of an Allied victory, an independent Armenia would be established in Cilicia and the five villayets (provinces) of Eastern Turkey.) Arabia would be given to the Arabs, Smyrna and its environs to the Greeks, and the Isle of Rhodes to the Italians. With Istanbul as its capital, a miniscule Turkey in the interior of Anatolia would be left for the Turkish people. Armenians were divided as to which of the victorious powers should be selected for the Armenian mandate, (the champion in the West of the Armenian cause, President Wilson, fell seriously ill at the critical moment of arranging an American protectorate) but, for the most part, Armenians were full of hope, and, anticipating independence after six centuries of Turkish domination, they began to reestablish businesses, to repair and build homes and to cultivate farms and vineyards. In October of 1919, the British Forces in Marash were replaced by the French, primarily Senegalese troops led by French officers, abetted by an Armenian contingent. Unbeknownst to the Armenians, dissension between the Allies had led the British (in an incredibly perverse ploy) to turn over to the Turks arms and ammunition with which to harass the French. During the period of the French occupation, rumors of hope and doom alternated within the Armenian community, but ended tragically in the sudden desertion of the French, leaving the Armenians helpless to defend themselves.

CHAPTER 7

DICRAN BERBERIAN'S MEMOIR

The best revenge is to be unlike him who performed the injury.
—Marcus Aurelius

Dicran Berberian, a cousin of my mother and her siblings was seventeen years old in 1920. Years later he recalled and wrote of his experiences of the Battle of Marash and afterwards which are both riveting and heartbreaking at the same time.

Dicran Berberian gave his papers in 1973 to his niece, Telma Trimmer, nee Berberian, and her husband, Robert Whitfield Trimmer, Ph.D., in 1973 in Loudonville, New York. The following three excerpts are from a document written in June 1969 by Dicran entitled "Dicran Abraham Berberian, M.D.: His Life and Family":

The Battle of Marash, January to March 1920
(by D.A. Berberian, M.D., an eyewitness)

In the city of Marash there were no strictly Christian or Muslim quarters. Nevertheless, in certain districts, especially in the vicinity of churches, the majority of homes were inhabited by Armenians. In the quarter, known as "Sheikh Mahallesi" where my uncle's home was located, a conglomerate of homes with common walls were inhabited by Armenians. These homes had underground basements with walls two feet in thickness built of mud and straw bricks. Some houses had a second floor which was either built of the same type of material or of wood. Most roofs were flat roofs covered with wooden beams, set a foot apart. The beams were covered either with rough boards or dried reeds placed on top of the roof a layer of earth about a foot in thickness. To prevent leakage, it was necessary to climb up on the roof and roll it with a stone roller. After snowfall roofs had to be shoveled to prevent cave-ins. Narrow streets often became impassable from shoveled snow. The homes of the wealthy had pitched roofs which were covered with parallel rows of fluted bricks, laid concave side up at first, covered with a top row of bricks laid in reverse.

There were altogether nine guns of every description in the possession of the men in the quarter to which were added the four guns of the wounded French soldiers. With these 13 guns the quarter was protected night and day. Here and there slanted slit-like openings were dug in the walls for the muzzles of shotguns and for observation. In order to let the Turkish neighbors, know that people were armed several blank shots were fired.

After the secret visit of a representative of Mustafa Kemal Pasha (later known as Ataturk) to Marash in the fall of 1919, incidents and disagreements between the Commander of the French Expeditionary Forces and the Turkish governmental authorities became more frequent. It was evident that the bands of Turks known as "chetes" were being organized to harass the French in preparation for guerilla warfare.

To represent the interests of Armenians a local Committee was organized under the Chairmanship of the Rev. Aram Bagdikian. Daily it became evident that the allied powers united in war were being torn apart in peace because of conflicting national interests. Armenians were being assured daily that the mighty and victorious French forces would assure the security of all people, Christians and Muslim, in the occupied territories, the jubilation of Armenians for total independence from six centuries of oppression by Turks began to appear premature. Voices of the wise raised to hush provocations against the Turkish community remained unheeded.

With entry into 1920 gloom on the political horizon became daily more intense. However, many optimistic Armenians still believed that an armed confrontation between the French Expeditionary Forces and the Turkish irregulars was unthinkable and would certainly result in the final subjugation of the Turks and the destruction of the Ottoman Empire, once and for all time.

The Christmas of 1920 was celebrated by Armenians as usual on January 18 with much foreboding. Schools were closed for a two-week period in celebration of Christmas, therefore, children were at home. For almost three months, shootings and quarrels had resulted in the closing of shops and a withdrawal of the population, Christians and Muslims, to their homes.

On that fateful morning of January 21, 1920 despite the entreaties of my mother for me to stay home, I took my younger brother Haroutune with me and together we went downtown, convincing my parents that if shops were closed we would soon return home. When we arrived downtown we found the shops closed and there were very few people in the marketplace. I just opened one portion of my store and stood in the doorway and served the few customers who came to shop much amazed that I had dared to keep my shop open when all shops were closed. At about 10 a.m. a French sentry appeared and asked me what we were doing downtown on such a critical day. The sergeant in charge of the sentry knew me and advised me to close my shop and return home.

I closed my shop but instead of returning home I decided to visit the Latin Church where a garrison of French troops was stationed, to better inform myself about the situation from the French lieutenant Cappanole, stationed with whom I was friendly. We arrived at the Latin Church on one of the seven hills on which the city of Marash was built at about 11 a.m. I met my friend the lieutenant as planned and was told that the situation was very critical as they were expecting trouble very soon. He advised me to go home. He assured me that the French forces were adequate to meet all exigencies, saying that sentries were everywhere in the city to protect people.

Thus about noon time we left the Latin Church and stopped on our way home at my uncle's home. My uncle, Hagop Agha Shamlian, was a well-known tanner in Marash. My aunt was preparing fresh bread and asked me to stay for lunch. As we had finished lunch and were getting ready to go home we heard a shot fired. It was about 1 p.m.

Our home was in the Divanli quarter about ten minutes of walking distance from where we were. In the Divanli quarter the majority of the inhabitants were Turks. Two of our neighbors were Turks and our home shared common walls with them from the south and west. Our neighbors to the east and north of our home were Armenians but their homes were separated from ours by a street and an alley way. Further south of our home was a small mosque and then a small market known as "Divanli Charshisi," further down and to the left was a public bath, the "Divanli Hamami."

The home of my uncle was in "Sheikh Mahallesi" and was a quarter inhabited largely by Armenians and was situated close to the Armenian Protestant First Church of Marash. My future father-in-law, Dr. Vartan Poladian's home was in this quarter. Because of the shooting from minarets and from the Turkish fortress in the center of the city, people everywhere descended to the basements of their homes for shelter. My uncle's home was an adobe house built of unburned mud and straw bricks with a wooden second floor where the bedrooms were. In the basement there was a private bath. We all huddled into the bathroom, two of us, my uncle, my aunt and their two sons, Hrant (an epileptic) and Toros.

It did not take us long to realize that war between the Turkish irregulars and the French troops had indeed started because cannons were being fired and conflagrations were starting in different parts of the city set up by Turks, and possibly by the French.

Communication between neighbors was soon established by boring through the contiguous walls and digging trenches across narrow alleys. There were about 700 people in the quarter where we were and it was estimated that there was a total of a dozen guns of assorted vintage. To protect the quarter against intrusion a local command was established and people with guns were assigned to their respective posts.

Word came that soon after shooting began Dr. Poladian's wife, Leah Hanum Poladian, was shot and killed instantly. The family of Poladians had descended to the basement and she had gone up, entered their parlor to bring down some pillows and was shot through their picture window facing the fortress.

We also heard that right outside the quarter four French soldiers on sentry duty were shot and the wounded were dragged into an Armenian home across the street. They needed the services of a doctor but there was no one able to communicate with them. Dr. Poladian, having lost his beloved wife was in tears and mourning, and was in no condition to leave his home and venture across the street to attend to the wounded. He said he would take care of them if they were brought in. The men in the quarter were on the lookout for one who could speak French and I was picked to be their emissary and interpreter. The leader of the defenders of the quarter picked four young men to go with me to the house across the street to bring in the wounded with their guns and ammunition and the inhabitants of the house.

After shouting to the neighbors across the street from the nearest home asking them to leave the gate open we ventured out on the street. As we ran across it several shots were fired at us, one of the bullets whizzed past my left ear and hit the wall. We dashed through the open door unhurt and were taken in. I told the soldiers that we had come to take them to a more easily defensible place where there was a doctor to take care of them. Two of the four sentries were black Senegalese. We waited for the nightfall and then dashed across the street. The wounded were carried on the backs of the young men.

We hoped against hope that the war would end in a few days, but alas fighting became more intense as days passed, fires illuminating the night sky. It was an exceptionally cold winter in Marash that year. It drizzled, rained or snowed most of the time and the temperature hovered around the freezing point at night. As the days passed by and ammunition dwindled it became necessary to establish lines of communication between the quarter and the nearest French outpost stationed in the Latin Church on the hill across the valley known as "Kanli Dere," blood valley. I was asked to write a note to the commander of the outpost and inform him that we were a group of 700 people in the quarter across the hill and had with us four wounded French soldiers. Although we had adequate food supplies we had exhausted our ammunition for the few guns of every description in our possession. We would need a contingent of soldiers with ammunition for our protection. A nine-year-old boy who knew the way was picked to slip across the valley in the dark of the night to carry the note to the outpost. He returned the same night and told us that he banged at the gate of the church which was opened and he was taken in. He brought back a message in which the commander stated that he was hopeful that the fighting would end soon, that reinforcements were awaited and until then he could not afford to send out soldiers from his outpost.

Days passed and no help was forthcoming. There were those among us who wanted to remain in their homes waiting, but the majority wished to flee to the Latin Church to enjoy the protection of the outpost. It never occurred to any one that the French forces could be vanquished by the Turkish irregulars. On the eighth day of the war, I was asked to write a second note to the commander telling him that our ammunition was exhausted and we had no choice but run over to the Latin church the following night and we would bring with us the four wounded soldiers. The message was remitted by the same boy who returned with a note that they would be on the lookout for us and would shell the neighboring Turkish quarter to prevent them from shooting at us.

On January 30, 1920 at about 8 p.m. all the people in the quarter assembled in the homes nearest the valley with whatever belongings one would be able to carry on his back. My brother and I took a small quilt each and as much raisins, figs, and bread as we could carry. We rushed down the valley, walked through to the stream of cold water, climbed the hill on the side opposite, ran through the empty streets and reached the gate of the Latin Church panting. The gate was opened for us. We entered the yard of the church. The church proper which could seat more than a thousand was packed with people who had taken refuge long before our arrival. The priests took us to the school building and assigned us a place in the corridor large enough for people to sit together huddled up for warmth.

The little food that we had brought with us was soon exhausted. Counting the soldiers, French forces mostly Algerian 210 in number, the Seminarians and the people who had taken refuge, there were altogether more than three thousand mouths to feed. Food supplies were soon exhausted. Marauding parties were organized to enter at night the neighborhood houses, Christian or non-Christian, in search of food. A soup kitchen was established and once a day a thin soup was distributed to the people for their nourishment.

The war continued unabated but it soon became evident that the Turks had also evacuated their homes and had taken their families to the neighboring villages. There were left here and there groups of armed chetes (guerillas) in the city shooting at the French outposts. Word came from the observation post on the bell tower of the Latin church that several churches in the city were set on fire. It was learned later that rags soaked in kerosene were thrown over the walls into the homes and churches to set them on fire.

On the fifteenth day of the war, the French flag was hoisted on all outposts where French troops were stationed to let the reinforcements encamped outside the city know not to bombard their own Thereupon, they bombarded the parts of the city but to the amazement of everyone they chose not to enter the city but remained in the outskirts. It became known after the war that the commander had decided to retreat without obtaining the authorization of the General Quérette.

February 1920 was a cold month and was ushered in with a heavy fall of snow. On the 19th day of the war on February 8, an aeroplane flew over the city in the afternoon. Everyone rejoiced thinking that the French were sending reinforcements to strengthen their garrisons. Several days later it became known that the aeroplane had dropped a message from General Gouraud, the commander of French Forces, to General Quérette, ordering him to evacuate the city. The sinister message was kept secret from Armenians. Feverish activity among the troops stationed in the Latin church became noticeable at once. They seemed to be gathering their belongings. We, the Armenians, were told that the soldiers were getting ready for maneuvers. The following day, on the 9th of February, at about 6:00 (or 7:00) p.m. the gate was opened and the troops began to walk out with their belongings. Were they going out for maneuvers or were they retreating? And if they were retreating should we or should we not flee with them?

Suddenly the cloud laden sky was aflame with explosions. We could not comprehend what was happening but those who had climbed the steeple of the church reported that the explosions were in the barracks north of the city occupied by the French.

My uncle, with many others, decided to pursue the retreating French soldiers. Two hours after the departure of French troops, we succeeded after much entreaties to any of those Armenians who had taken charge, to let us out of the Latin church. We walked in the snow through trenches, entered the German Hospital; filled with wounded French and Turkish soldiers and under the care of the American Near East Relief Organization (NER). We came out through a breech in the northern wall of the hospital and through trenches proceeded toward the American College for Girls. There we soon learned that indeed all French troops had evacuated, and set fire to the left over ammunition and their last contingents had departed two hours before our arrival.

Miss Blakely, the Directress of the College met us at the gate and told us that she would not take in able bodied men but would give shelter to women and children. My uncle asked me to flee with him in pursuit of the French troops. I told him I would not. He asked me if I had any money with me, I said, yes I did, but it wasn't much. I handed him my purse and told him that I would stay behind for my feet were wet, almost frozen, from the cold. I was shivering and was poorly dressed. If I walked a few more hours in the cold I would freeze to death. I said, I'll take my chances and stay. I thought to myself, I know several prominent Turks and perhaps they would intervene on my behalf and I would not be slaughtered.

My uncle bade us, and his wife and children, goodbye and walked out with other able bodied men and women into a heavy snow storm. He finally reached Adana with frozen toes, several of which had to be amputated there. It was later learned that out of a group of over three thousand men and women who had elected to follow in the trail of the retreating French troops, many had frozen on their way. Many mothers who had taken their children with them were forced to abandon them in a half frozen dazed state to die in the snow.

On February 11, 1920, a strange atmosphere fell upon the people remaining in the girl's college. It was said that the day before a Turk, Dr. Mustafa had come with a white flag to meet the Commander of the French Troops with the express purpose of seeking terms for peace. As he was returning from his interview he was shot somewhere in or near the German Hospital. It was surmised that the French Commander after receiving the Turkish emissary had told him that he was under instruction to withdraw. It is not unlikely, therefore, that an Armenian who knew of it shot the man in order to give a breathing spell to those who had opted to follow the French troops.

The retreat of the French troops came as a total surprise to the Turks. They could hardly believe it for it was not until several days later that they began to infiltrate the city from their hideouts in the mountains. The war of Marash was the beginning of the Turkish resistance against the French and later on against the Greeks. It ushered in the era of Mustafa Kemal Pasha, the Ataturk. This resistance spread from Marash to Ourfa (Urfa/Edessa the original Greek name], Hadjin, Beredjik, Aintab, Tarsus, Adana and other towns and cities throughout Cilicia.

$$* \qquad * \qquad *$$

My First Outing After the War of Marash
(written by D.A. Berberian, M.D. in 1969)

Three weeks after the desertion of the French Expeditionary Forces and cessation of hostilities in Marash on March 2, 1920, two Americans, Doctors R. (Robert) A. Lambert and Dr. Lorrin Shephard, officers of the Near East Relief organization, came to the city for an objective evaluation of the situation.

Dr. Marion Wilson of the Near East Relief organization, stationed in Marash, looked for someone who knew the city, spoke English and would be willing to serve as a guide to the two doctors to observe the ravaged condition of the city. Up to that date no Armenian had yet dared to go out from their several sanctuaries for fear of being shot or killed. Dr. Wilson asked me if I would go with them. I accepted to do so thinking that both doctors being American and in uniform no one would dare to shoot at me or at them.

We started the tour from the American Mission complex. On our way we stopped at our home, halfway between the mission complex and Bett Shallum, the former German orphanage for boys. Although I had suspected that my parents, (Mr. Abraham Berberian and Mrs. Shamiram Berberian) were perhaps killed, as our home was in a quarter largely inhabited by Muslims, I still hoped against hope that they could be alive hiding somewhere. The gate to our home was wide open and our household effects were carried away. The only things remaining were some of my father's books and writings, which were thrown into the mud in the yard. I salvaged our family Bible and a few pictures.

We then proceeded towards the campus of the Armenian Protestant First Church which was burnt as well as the four adjacent buildings: Grade School and Parsonage, Kindergarten and Nursery, the Middle School and the Boys' Academy. We saw no dead bodies in this church and in its surroundings. Those who had sought refuge at this church had fled to the bottom of the hill to the Armenian Catholic Church, where there was an outpost of French regulars. We then proceeded towards the market place. All the shops were broken open and plundered, including my grocery store.

We walked through the length of the main market to the Armenian Gregorian Church at the southern end of the city known as the "Karasoun Mangantz." The church was burnt to the ground and we saw here and there charred bodies. We then proceeded westward towards another Gregorian Church known as "Sourp Asdvatzatzin" (St. Mary's) which was also burned. Two of the outer walls of this church were contiguous with adobe and frame houses with flat roofs. Many homes in this district constituted a conglomerate of homes in that houses were stuck together. These homes were inhabited entirely by Armenians. All those homes were burned by Turks who had thrown in flaming rags soaked in kerosene. The inhabitants of these homes must have flocked into the adjoining church to better protect themselves. The conflagration must have reached the church and set it aflame.

We entered St Mary's Church and felt sick. The stench of partly charred naked bodies was a nauseating and despicable sight. Naked corpses were everywhere but hundreds were piled at the altar where evidently many had fallen on top of another. As none of the men or women had rings on their fingers or jewelry of any kind, it was more likely that marauding Turks had come in, robbed the corpses of jewelry and money and piled them one on top of another at the altar.

From St. Mary's we went to the Second Armenian Protestant Church which was also burned. We then walked towards the "Seray." the government building which was intact and we did not enter in. From thence we came to the Third Armenian Protestant Church which was also burnt and returned to the American Mission Compound having concluded a circular tour of the city.

*   *   *

How My Family Was Annihilated
(written by D.A. Berberian, M.D. in 1969)

In May 1920 I got a job as a pharmacy boy in the German Hospital where the doctors of the Near East Relief Organization treated the wounded Turkish and French soldiers. I was to help Mr. Stepan Tehorbadjian, the pharmacist. I enjoyed my work tremendously. There was a U.S. Dispensatory in the pharmacy which I began to read and study. I learned much about drugs, their uses and toxicity. In August of that year, the pharmacist came down with a severe case of typhoid fever and was hospitalized for two months. In the absence of any other qualified person I was permitted to do the dispensing.

One day a young Turkish fellow came to the pharmacy with a prescription to be filled. I immediately recognized him for he lived in the house adjacent to ours. I asked him if my parents were at home during the Marash War and whatever happened to them. He told me that they were at home at the beginning of the war but on the 3rd or 4th day they left their home and congregated with their neighbors in another home near the cemetery on the eastern side of the town. He said, "We besieged the place where they were hiding and threatened to burn the house, but did not dare to do so because the adjacent home belonged to Turks." He said, "We finally broke in and found a group of 50 or more people, men, women and children, huddled together in one room. Your father asked permission to read from a book and to pray before surrendering. We let him do so. He stood up, read and prayed and then we slaughtered them all, men, women and children. We wouldn't waste our bullets on them. We smashed the heads of the children against the wall and killed the men and women with axes and hoes. If you do not believe what I am saying is true here is the proof."

At that moment he took out of his pocket a silver pocket watch which I immediately recognized as my father's. He also told me that my father had a small Browning with six cartridges. It was true for I knew he had a Browning with six cartridges; none was used. After killing them they must have robbed them. I asked then what had happened to the bodies. He said that they dumped them all in a ditch.

I knew he was telling the truth for early in March 1920 about a month after the termination of the war, Armenians were permitted to go out and look for their dead and bury them if they cared to. At that time several of our neighbors who had fled to Bett Shallum and had survived asked me and my brother, Haroutune, to accompany them to identify the bodies of our loved ones and bury them properly. I couldn't bring myself to join them in the search but they went anyway and found the naked bodies dumped in a ditch. They said that many of the corpses were unidentifiable; those whom they recognized as their own they picked up and buried and covered the ditch with soil. There in that ditch remain unto this day the broken bodies of my parents, my two sisters, Lousatzin (thirteen years old) and Angele (eleven years old) and my youngest brother, Emmanuel (six years old).

Naturally I was quite upset having listened to the shocking narrative. My eyes were filled with tears and the thought came to my mind that if I mixed some arsenious oxide in the quinine cachets I was preparing for him I would perhaps revenge myself. I thought I could do this very easily for I was alone in the pharmacy and was accountable to no one. Then the thought came to my mind that my father would be the first to condemn me; he would not condone such an action even against those who had slaughtered mercilessly helpless women and children.

When I regained my senses there was only pity in my heart for those despicable people who had committed the atrocities.

$*$ $*$ $*$

Raffi Berberian writes in 1988 in *A Remembrance of My Parents: Dicran and Armine Berberian*:

Thus was my father orphaned at the age of sixteen and left to care for his younger brother. It was fortunate that he was energetic and adaptable by nature and had been raised to work hard. Though yet an adolescent, he had learned to be resourceful. In school and on the street, he had become conversant in German, then French and English, in addition to his native Armenian and Turkish, and, over the years, he had made himself indispensable to the successive foreign soldiers and missionaries, acting as their guide, errand boy, interpreter and procurer of supplies. Whatever shyness he may have felt, he quickly overcame, and my father, who stood no taller than 5' 1", never allowed his lack of physical stature, his sudden poverty or the bitterness of having lost his family to intimidate him or to discourage him from reaching for the highest goals. He would try harder. He would excel. He was a survivor.

And so did my mother, at the age of twelve, lose her beloved mother. A year later, her father, Dr. Poladian, married a recently widowed schoolteacher with an infant son, the former Araxie Haidostian, a remarkable woman of intellect, high bearing and iron fortitude, who as my step-grandmother was to be the only grandparent I would know. Her first husband, the Reverend Nerses Kouyoumjian, was among the many clergymen killed in the Massacre of Adana while attending the Conference of Evangelical Ministers. This ruthless act by the Turkish authorities was intended to cripple the burgeoning Evangelical movement by stripping the church of its leadership.

My parents' Christian faith has been sufficient to forgive their oppressors. Having suffered at the hands of the Turks, perhaps as much as any, they long ago became truly free of those who had persecuted them by banishing revenge-seeking hate from their hearts. Although, as a child, I knew that my grandparents had been killed in a war, it was not until my teens that I became acquainted with the full story of the atrocities, and this I learned from other children of American Armenians. When I confronted my parents with this gap in my education, they explained that they had intended to give me these details in time, but not until they felt I was sufficiently mature to understand them in historical context, wishing to spare me the curse of ignorant hatred for the people of any nation. As I grew older, my parents did in fact encourage me to read books about the genocide, and they became willing to satisfy my curiosity and share details of their past.

CHAPTER 8
LIVES OF DICRAN
AND ARMINE BERBERIAN:
AFTER THE BATTLE OF MARASH

From *A Remembrance of My Parents: Dicran and Armine Berberian* written by Raffi Berberian in 1988:

In 1922, four years after the end of World War I, the reformist Turkish government offered to the remaining Armenians the option to emigrate in return for the surrender of their rights and property.

My father had sold his parents' house, and when the Government made emigration possible for the Armenians, he arranged to get himself and his brother to Beirut, Lebanon, where he hoped to pursue a medical education. He began by looking up an old friend and former mentor, Dr. Triandaphilo Ladakis, a pharmacist on the faculty of the American University, who, because of his Greek ancestry had been exiled during the war years by the Turkish government to relative banishment in Marash in the Turkish interior. Although without financial resources and relatives able to offer financial assistance, my father managed to put himself through the American University of Beirut, graduating cum laude both from college and medical school. Two examples of my father's creative initiative and flexibility come quickly to mind. While in college, with the support of Dr. Bayard Dodge, the President of the American University, and Professor L. H. Seelye, my father initiated and directed "cooperative clubs" enabling needy students like himself (50 to 60 at a time) to live together and share expenses. This precedent-setting venture made college accessible to many who otherwise would have been denied access to higher education. In my childhood, I recall meeting numerous grateful men, family friends newly arrived from Lebanon who had known my father as the pioneering student whose trailblazing efforts had made possible for them opportunities otherwise unthinkable. In his youth, my father had enjoyed playing the violin, and so, in college, with Edward Khendamian, he organized a student orchestra, switching to the cello when no one else in the group was willing to take up that instrument. He used music as a bond to bring together individuals of different backgrounds. It is no wonder that the University authorities valued him for his brilliance, initiative and charismatic leadership.

There had been three Armenian Protestant Churches in Marash. Both my parents' families had been affiliated with the First Church, and my father remembered my mother as a little girl in Sunday school, daughter of the distinguished doctor for whom he had had the greatest respect. My father also remembered my mother as the little sister of his friend, Aram, both boys having played violin together in school. My mother, travelling from Syria to California in the company of Helen Shamlian, a cousin of my father's, had the occasion to become reacquainted with my father when, prior to setting sail, he gave his cousin and her companion a tour of Beiruit. He was handsome and very much the man about town, and when he began to correspond with my mother across the ocean, she responded positively. Their correspondence developed into love letters and an engagement by mail.

After a difficult year teaching Mexican-American children in grade school, my mother set sail for Beirut to meet her bridegroom. My parents were married on Christmas Eve, 1932, in the American Presbyterian Church in Beirut. The Reverend Yenouk Geokgeuzian and my father's mentor, Professor Seelyre, officiated.

As a teacher in the Department of Microbiology of the Medical School of the American University, my father distinguished himself, and he was awarded a Rockefeller Fellowship in 1935-1936 for postgraduate studies in parasitology, medical mycology, and malariology at the London School of Tropical Medicine and Hygiene, the Universite de Paris and the Instituto di Anita Pubblica in Rome. He was Instructor in bacteriology and parasitology at the School of Medicine of the American University of Beirut, 1930-1935; Adjunct Professor of bacteriology and parasitology, 1936-1945; Associate Professor of bacteriology and chairman of the department from 1945-1947.

In the early 1930's, Beirut was an idyllic city. The beauty of its natural setting along the seashore in West Beirut was enhanced by the construction of spacious European-style villas with magnificent landscaped gardens. In 1938, my parents had a beautiful house custom-built to their specifications.

To relieve the exigencies of the Second World War when supplies from the outside world were cut off, my father and his colleague, Dr. E. W. Dennis, the Chairman of the Department of Bacteriology, were directed by the Lebanese Government and the American University to produce serums and vaccines for human and veterinary use in Lebanon and neighboring countries. There was an urgent need for anti-malarial control among recent immigrants of Armenian heritage. Immediately prior to World War II, the French Occupation Forces had withdrawn from the Turkish region of Sandjak of Alexandretta where over 100,000 Armenians lived. These inhabitants were permitted to take with them the equivalent of 25 Turkish paper pounds to be resettled (by the French forces) in Syria and in the three most malarial regions of Lebanon, namely the outskirts of Tyre, the Beirut River area and Ainjar in the Bekaah Valley. The French were precluded from fulfilling their promise to provide adequate housing when their government fell to the Germans early in the War, so these refugees were left to survive in white cloth tents. Pernicious malaria soon reached epidemic proportions. At the request of President Bayard Dodge of the American University and with the participation of the Armenian General Benevolent Union, my father initiated control measures against this devastating outbreak. Efforts were undertaken to destroy the mosquitoes' breeding places in the stagnant waters encircling the settlements. President Dodge obtained the requisite financial support for this operation from Mihran Karagheusian, a leading rug merchant in New York. Within three months, the epidemic was under control, not only in the Armenian camps, but in the neighboring Arab villages as well. With the help of squadrons of medical students, thousands of school children in the Levant were vaccinated against smallpox, typhus, plague, typhoid and paratyphoid fevers. In 1935, through his research on oriental sore (also called Aleppo button), my father discovered an inoculation procedure. In the process of mass vaccination against typhus fever in Syria, my father himself contracted the disease, but thanks to having been vaccinated previously, he recovered. These heroic efforts earned for him the Gold Medal of the Republic of Lebanon.

In 1928, the Reverend Yenovk Hadidian established in the Lebanese village of Maamektein a sanatorium for the treatment of tuberculosis for Armenian refugees. Thereafter, my father, along with others, including Dr. Hovsep Yeni-Komshian and Mr. Jacob Kunstler, founded nearby the Armenian National Sanatorium of Lebanon as a successor institution. They soon made plans for a modern facility which was built in the clean air of Azounieh in the Lebanon Mountains. My father served as Secretary of the Board of Directors of this institution. (After emigrating to the United States, he assumed the chairmanship of the American Board of Directors.) From 1935 until he left Beirut in 1947, he served as Chairman of the Armenian Evangelical College of Beirut. From 1941 until 1947, my father was a member of the Municipal Council of the City of Beirut. He served as advisor on malaria control and sanitation to the Near East Foundation from 1945 until 1947. Prior to his emigration from Lebanon in 1947, Dr. Berberian was the assistant director of the hospital laboratories at the American University of Beirut, 1935-1946, a co-founder of the American Sanitorium of Lebanon and the Secretary of the Board of Directors of the Sanitorium, 1931-1947.

Under the guidance and encouragement of Dr. Dodge, with funds from Miss Leila Karagheusian, and in collaboration with his colleague, Dr. Yeni-Komshian, he founded the Howard Karagheusian Child Welfare Centers of Bourj

Hammoud and Ainjar, Lebanon and served as the secretary of the Board of Directors from 1942 until 1947.

With the birth of my sister, Cynthia, in 1937, my mother discovered a new fulfillment. She took enormous pleasure in decking out her daughter in the prettiest dresses. Three years later, my parents had a son, Dicran Aram, followed by me, Raffi Robert, born in 1944.

Through the good offices of his former colleague, Dr. E.W. Dennis (and much benevolent encouragement from Mrs. Dennis), who had joined the staff of the Sterling-Winthrop Research Institute, the research facility of the Sterling Drug Company, a way was found for our family to emigrate to the United States. Upon the invitation of Dr. Maurice L. Tainter, the Director of the Institute in Rensselaer, New York, a suburb of Albany, my father joined that institution as a Senior Investigator, beginning (in 1947) a thirty-year career with the Company. Immigration to the U.S. was also made possible by the simultaneous invitation of the Albany Medical College of Union University to my father to teach medical parasitology and to perform research on the chemotherapy of parasitic diseases.

My father and mother were the last of their immediate families to leave the Old Country for the New World. My mother's sister, Zabel, had left Beirut with her family to resettle in Brazil in 1938, and, in 1939, my father's brother, Haroutune and his family also emigrated to Brazil.

Upon arrival in New York in August 1947, our family was embraced by my mother's sister, Azniv, and her husband, the Reverend Mr. Samuel Rejebian.

My father found a four-bedroom house in Loudonville, a suburb of Albany, situated directly north of the city.

The director of Sterling-Winthrop, Dr. Tainter, wanted my father to become physician of the Institute in addition to his activities in research of chemotherapy of tropical diseases, so my father spent ten days preparing for the exam and received his license to practice medicine in New York. Since 1947, Dr. Berberian was associated with Sterling-Winthrop Research Institute, the research facility of the Sterling Drug Company. He began as a Senior Investigator, 1947-1949; then a Member, 1950; Member and Director of the Medical

Department, 1950-1956; Senior Member and Director of the Medical Department, 1956-1961; Senior Research Associate (Biology), Staff Physician, 1962-1969, and since 1969, he was Consultant to the Medical Department.

Behind the Loudonville house was a large garage building with an apartment above. In December 1948, my father began a private practice in the garage apartment, seeing patients on evenings and Saturdays. (One of his first patients was the mother of George Deukmejian, later to become Governor of California.)

Dr. Berberian joined the faculty of the Albany Medical College, Albany, New York, a division of Union University in 1947 as Assistant Clinical Professor of Medicine; from 1956-1965, he was Associate Professor and 1965-1968, he was Professor of Microbiology at the Albany Medical College. He also served as a consultant in medicine to the Veterans Administration Hospital in Albany from 1953-1968.

Dr. Berberian was the co-discoverer of several new drugs for the treatment of malaria (Plaquenil), amebiasis (Milibis-Aralen, Mantomide, Falmonox), and schtosomiasis (Etrenol or Hycathone).

He was known worldwide as an authority on chemotherapy of malaria and schistosomiasis—two of the commonest parasitic diseases which were known to infect hundreds of millions of people.

CHAPTER 9

RECOLLECTIONS OF
ARTHUR S. YERANIAN

*What lies behind us and what lies before us are tiny matters
compared to what lies within us.*
—Ralph Waldo Emerson

Arthur S. Yeranian was born on February 22, 1910 and died on April 5, 1992. He was born in Marash, Turkey to Avedis Yeranian and Nazender Charhudian Yeranian. The story of Arthur Yeranian's family of Marash is typical of most Armenians of the Ottoman Empire pre-1915. They were ordinary, hard-working people, dedicated to their families and to their respective churches, whether they were Apostolic, Catholic, or Protestant.

The district of Alemli was located at the southeast section of Marash. Armenian and Turkish homes were side by side and Christians and Muslims lived there, often peacefully. The wealthy had two-story houses with gardens, fountains, and tiled roofs. While those with modest means had homes with flat roofs, drab courtyards, and no fountains. This type of home was similar to the dwelling of Arthur Yeranian's family.

In the year 1855 (when Franklin Pierce was president of the United States), Arthur's grandfather, Sarkis—who was of medium build, square face and ruddy complexion—married. Turvand, his bride, was fourteen years old. She had fair skin and dark brown eyes.

Sarkis was a weaver of cotton fabrics. After they married and as a diversion from her innumerable household chores, Turvand spun fabrics herself. Their family grew and eventually they had three sons and four daughters. Their eldest son, Hagop, was born in 1856. At thirteen years of age, Hagop helped his father at the loom. He also had a beautiful voice which at puberty changed into a somber baritone. Hagop began singing solos on Sundays at Saint Sarkis Apostolic Church. During the Mass when he sang, "Lord, have mercy upon us," the coppersmith, Nishan, was so moved that he offered Hagop an apprenticeship at his store. He accepted the position and, because he so loved learning, he also attended night school. In 1882, he graduated from the Central Academy. Subsequently, he enrolled at the local American Theological Seminary that had recently relocated to Marash from Aintab. He graduated in 1886 and eventually became a minister of the Gospel. For many years, he preached the Word in Afrion-Karahissar and Smyrna.

Markarid, Sarkis and Turvand's first daughter, was born in 1859. She had hazel eyes and a beautiful crop of red hair. When she was barely fourteen, she married the son of the Atamian family. Avedis, born in 1864, would eventually be Arthur's father. He had a large forehead, light-brown hair, and light-brown eyes. Using the family bible as a textbook, Sarkis taught Avedis to read. The family library consisted of an heirloom bible, in ancient Armenian, a book of prayers by Naregatsi, and elementary arithmetic written in Turkish, and a Turkish first-year reader with Arabic characters.

The couple's second daughter was born in 1866. She was named Vartehr (or Vartig), translated Rosa or "Little Rose." She had large blue eyes, brown hair, and a round face. Vartehr turned down all the handsome young men who asked for her hand in marriage.

During the same year of Vartehr's birth, 1866, Grandfather Sarkis changed from the Apostolic form of worship to the Evangelical. When Miriam was born in 1869, she was the first in the family to be baptized at the Divanli Evangelical Church with Reverend Murad Gulesserian officiating. When Miriam graduated from the American Girls' College in 1890, she had a good command of the English language. Dr. Thomas Christie (a missionary scholar) hired her to be his secretary and translator. On August 6, 1897, Miriam came to the United States and later married John Bayerian, a steel-mill employee in Syracuse, New York. Miriam was very helpful to members of her own family.

Vartan was born in August of 1870. He was the youngest and handsomest of the three sons. He graduated from Aintab College in 1898 and then attended the Marash Theological Seminary. He also was ordained a minister of the Gospel. He married Nuvart Halebian of Aintab and soon after was assigned to the preaching of the Word in the town of Deort Yol.

Yestehr (Esther) was born in 1877. She was the last child and the fourth daughter of the family. She became a teacher in the elementary schools sponsored by both English and German missionaries. As a teacher, she met another teacher by the name of Hovhannes Haidostian. They married and raised a good-sized family.

Making the transition from one form of worship—the Apostolic to Evangelical—was not an easy decision for Grandfather Sarkis. He had sharp disagreements with his brother Nazar, who would continue worshipping in the Apostolic Church. But Sarkis preferred, as he said, to talk with God directly without the necessity of mediation by a priest.

In 1878, Sarkis had a stroke that incapacitated him. His son, Avedis, was sixteen years old. There were eight mouths to feed. So Avedis sat at his loom from dawn till dusk, weaving cotton fabrics as fast as he could. Auntie Vartehr took charge of the housekeeping so that Grandmother Turvand had more time spinning yarn at the wheel.

After suffering five years of infirmity, Grandfather Sarkis passed away in 1883. His funeral was held at the Divanli Evangelical Church and was well attended by relatives, friends, including several Turkish neighbors, American missionaries, and certain members of the Apostolic Church.

Reverend Ohan Guydzakian delivered the eulogy and said of Sarkis, "...a man devoutly dedicated to harmony, mutual understanding, and unity." Sarkis had worked with Father Nahabed of the Apostolic Church to establish goodwill and understanding among the people of all faiths, whether they were Apostolics, Evangelicals, or Muslims.

The membership of the Evangelical Church was growing. When Avedis began teaching Sunday school, he knew more copies of the bible were needed. He would have to go to Constantinople to buy the bibles and religious pamphlets. He would become the main supplier of educational books in Marash. He was first of all a weaver and wanted to improve his weaving technique; but, to do so meant taking a trip to the seacoast town of Antioch. There he saw machines designed to weave stockings of all kinds. There were no such machines in Marash. Avedis spent a few weeks learning the mechanics and returned with two stocking weaving machines, complete with spare parts. He could now rent a store that displayed both stockings and books. He told people at his parish about his wish to find a store. One of the parishioners, Hagop Shamlian, a well-known tanner, offered to rent Avedis a store he owned that was close to the downtown shopping mall, Belediyeh Market.

It was a small store, with perhaps a twenty-foot frontage and a total of fifteen feet front to back. The glass door was in the front center, accessible by three steps up from the street. The rest of the front was also framed in glass, to make the store contents visible from the street. The stocking display cabinets were up against the left wall while the rear and the right walls were covered with all manner of educational books and bibles. It didn't take long for the store to become the center of knowledge-seeking customers, both Armenians and Turks. It was also attended by the well-to-do, who made a habit of wearing stockings.

Avedis was middle aged when he thought about marriage. Uncle Nazar and his wife, Haiganoush, were of the Apostolic faith and suggested the second daughter of Nishan, the coppersmith. But Avedis didn't like her, especially her voice. Then there was the youngest daughter of Nahabed Charhudian. He had joined the Evangelicals at the same time as Grandfather Sarkis. Nahabed was a dealer in chemicals, like sulfur, potash, and phosphorus.

The girl was Nazender. Two weeks after meeting her, engagement ceremonies were performed at Uncle Nazar's house. The wedding was simple, and Reverend Garabed Hartunian gave a short sermon advising the couple to be upright and God fearing at all times.

Within a year after the union of Avedis and Nazender, a daughter was born. Sadly, she got sick and died at six months of age. Three years after the daughter, a boy was born in 1907 and named Sarkis after Grandfather.

In 1910, the author of the memoir to follow, Arthur, was born. Then, a girl, Makrouhi (meaning purity) came along. Then a boy, Pavlos (Paul), was born in 1915.

In those days, German education was highly regarded. Teachers were very strict. Avedis wanted his sons, Paul and Arthur, to attend the school and orphanage known as Bett Shallum or "Beytchallum." It covered an area of perhaps eight to twelve acres with a main four-story building, dormitories, classrooms, an assembly hall, a yard for athletic activities, teachers' quarters, a large mess hall, and a kitchen. It was a boarding school for the orphans, as well as an elementary school for boys who commuted from their homes in Marash.

Arthur had not yet experienced any signs of Turkish hostility until the day he had to go to school alone. Someone hurled a stone at him, hitting his forehead with a sharp blow and narrowly missed his left eye. The perpetrator turned out to be Hassan, the son of their neighbor. Avedis confronted Hassan's father, who subsequently blamed the government for fermenting hatred toward the Armenians.

In 1915, even the children knew there was a war going on. But the Armenians did not know of the directives, which were sent out by the heads of the government—Talaat Bey, Enver Pasha, and Jemal Bey—to exterminate the Armenians.

One day in May 1915, Uncle Nazar went over to the home of Avedis, quite excited. He exclaimed, "Two gendarmes knocked at our door today. They told us to get ready by tomorrow morning to leave Marash. 'Yallah, sevkiyet!' they said. 'Come on! Get ready for deportation!'"

News came from all districts. At least one thousand Armenian families were so notified. There were a few who complained or rebelled. They were hanged immediately in full public view. Actual deportation of the initial contingent did not occur until Sunday afternoon. Uncle Nazar, Auntie Haiganoush, and children, the whole family left Avedis and his family with prayers and tears. As a carpenter, Uncle Nazar had worked hard to build and build and repair and repair. He had harmed no one.

Thereafter, every few weeks, groups of deportations took place until they reached a climax in mid-August. Quite often, only a few hours' notice was given. Each family had to make instant decisions about what to leave behind and what to take with them. Arthur's family was untouched that year.

Then, in the spring of 1916, on a beautiful day in May just after sunset, when Avedis had just arrived home, there came a knock at the door.

"Open! Police!"

Two gendarmes, heavily armed, walked in. "Get ready, Yeran Avedis. "We have orders for your deportation. You have till tomorrow morning. Yallah! Sevkiyet!"

Grandmother Turvand and Auntie Vartehr were permitted to remain at home. Arthur's brother, Sarkis, being three years older than Arthur, could be helpful to his parents on the way. So Avedis decided to take him along. Arthur must have looked too young and helpless. Father asked Auntie to take Arthur to the German orphanage soon after their departure. As for Arthur's sister, Makrouhi, Grandmother insisted on her remaining at home. Pavlos was a mere infant. He couldn't be left anywhere. He was to go with his parents.

And so it was that next morning, his parents, clutching onto a few bare necessities, accompanied by their eldest and youngest sons, were herded out of their ancestral home. Arthur was taken into the German orphanage to the kindergarten section of the dormitories. Only Arthur and his mother survived the deportations (1915-1916) and the Battle of Marash.

The excerpt that follows is taken from Arthur Yeranian's book, *The Civilized*, from the chapter entitled "A True Story":

Here I must end my mother's words, important as they are to me and to our posterity. Every time I hear mother speak of a portion of her experiences, I cannot bear to listen to it any more than a few minutes at a time. My heart begins to ache. My experiences in the German orphanage are another indelible record written on the other side of the same sheet. While Kaiser Wilhelm was flaunting his superiority and President Wilson was trying to avoid getting into the European conflict, the number of orphans was rapidly increasing at the orphanage. It was as if the German missionaries were expecting these developments. As early as 1909, the German Huls-Bund Society President Pastor Ernst Lomann had sent word to Marash to expand their orphanage facilities. Since August 1915, orphans had been pouring in not only from Marash and its outlying districts, but also from Zeytoon, a town beyond the mountains in the north.

I remember that a Herr Blank, carpenter by trade, was in charge of the orphanage. Since I was a gentle and obedient little boy, strict discipline and various types of regimentation did not annoy me as it might have other boys. I was known not by my name, but by the number they had assigned to me—#167—which was stamped on all my clothing and other belongings.

Every day at the same time we got up, washed up, put our clothes on and reported for breakfast, as regularly as the hour hand of a clock. We started classes at 8:00 A.M. with a hymn: "Jesu geforan, Auf der lebens ban..." Then we sang other songs:

> *Sum, Sum, Sum [pronounced Zum, zum, zum],*
> *Bienchen sum herum.*
> *Ei wir tun dir nicht zuleide,*
> *Fliegt nun als und Wald und heide,*
> *Sum, Sum, Sum,*
> *Bienchen sum herum.*

Across the passage of at least sixty years' time, I can state only what I remember, without looking up any reference books to correct my mistakes. I remember more of the melodies than I do the words:

Wo findet, die Seek, die Heimat, die Ruh,
Wer denkt sie mit...fitischen zu...
Nein, nein, nein, nein; dieses allein.
Kann ruhplatz und Heimat, der sele nur sein.

...Lieb Heimatland ade...

...Hinaus in die Ferne mit...

...Ich hat einen Kameraten...

Deutschland, Deutschland, fiber alles,
Über alles in der Welt...
Deutsche Frauen, Deutsche Treue,
Deutscher wein und Deutscher sein.

Of course, at Christmas time we were taught a whole new group of songs.

Stille Nacht, heilige Nacht, Alles schleft, einsam wacht...
O du frohliche, O du selige, Knaden bringen der
Weinachtzeit.
Es ist ein Reisensprungen...
O Tannenbaum, O Tannenbaum...
Frohliche Weinacht iiberall, T önet durchte lufte froher schal.

Need I list more?

Of all the activities, group singing had the most appeal to me. My voice was not particularly outstanding, but my ears were sensitive to quality as well as pitch variations. The German songs always came with the musical notes above the words. Before long I could sight-sing practically any song even if I had never heard it previously.

Most afternoons were spent in group gymnastics and military march formations. We were lined up in a row and given numbers such as ein, zwei, drei, vier, in repeated sequences. This divided us in four groups so that we might obey orders such as "Links urn kert!" "March!" in the well-known goosestep fashion.

Christmas time left us with the best of memories. In addition to indoor decorations, singing and other programs, we received gifts such as colorful handkerchiefs, oranges from Yaffa and Dceryol, and toys from Germany. I had been dreaming of a mouth harmonica for some time, and my dreams came true. I carried the precious instrument with me, and at night it was securely wrapped and hidden under my pillow.

But all such bliss was of a temporary nature. The tide of war was gradually turning against Germany. We could sense the gradual disappearance of minor luxuries we had enjoyed as orphans. Food became scarcer. We were given less and less to eat. The routine was just a small bowl of soup at noon (rarely with meat) and only a small piece of bread in the evening. Every other evening the morsel of bread was supplemented with a few raisins or other dried fruit. Salt became nonexistent, and we, too, were looking at the meadows in search of edible grass.

I suppose it was a most difficult and trying time for the German missionaries to realize that Germany could be defeated after all. Herr Blank became sick and died soon after he heard about the "shame" of German defeat and the signing of the Armistice treaty. When the Allies came to Syria and penetrated certain regions of Turkey, the American missionaries and the Near East Relief agencies took over the orphanage.

Marash was first occupied by the British and then the French. It was during this time that many of the Armenian deportees, who were still alive, returned to their ancestral homes. My mother and brother Sarkis came home from Aleppo and joined my grandmother, Auntie Vartehr, and my sister Makrouhi. Once again, the household was under one roof, except myself. I stayed in the orphanage because Mother had a difficult time in finding any livelihood. When she found something to do, it was as a seamstress in the American missionary compound.

On a Wednesday afternoon, late in January of 1920, we heard some gunshots. Some of the bullets were coming toward the orphanage from the nearby minaret. We were told the Turks had begun fighting the French. The conflict lasted three weeks and carried away with it many innocent bystanders. The Turks found ample opportunity to kill and to plunder and burn as many Armenians as they could. All of the Christian churches (five Apostolic and three Evangelical) were burned. Many stores were sacked and burned. In the District of Sheker-Dereh, in St. Kevork Church, where they had gathered all the women, children and the very elderly, every one was killed by the sword and thrown into the fire. In the church of Asdvadzadzin ("born of God") two thousand Christians and fifty French soldiers were burned to death.

When the French retreated, and the smoke cleared, among the killed were my seventy-seven-year-old Grandma Turvand, Auntie Vartehr, my sister Makroohi, and my brother Sarkis—the very boy who had suffered so much during deportation and, miraculously, had returned alive. Had God kept him alive just to have him killed a year later?

Since Mother was unable to return home on the day the conflict began, her life was spared by remaining in the American compound.

Who am I? During the so-called "formative" years I had little or nothing to be comforted by. As a child, my face was hardly ever wrinkled by a smile. The American missionaries seemed to be always smiling. I felt perhaps they were masking their true feelings.

It was good to know my uncles were concerned about my getting an education. Uncle Hagop was now preaching in a church in Smyrna. He wanted me to come there. But by the time my passport was ready, Smyrna fell into the hands of the Turks and my uncle passed away on his way to a rescue ship at the bay.

Then it was my Uncle Vartan. He was preaching in a church in Thessaloniki, Greece. Dr. George E. White of the American Board of Missions was about to open the Anatolia Preparatory School there. Having applied eight months prior to the opening date, I must have been one of the first, if not the first, to be accepted as a student.

I shall mention only some of the events that had a profound effect on my thinking, attitudes, philosophy, and beliefs. Love of good music had been my primary enjoyment in life. When I was fifteen, I sold my postage stamp collection for a price that enabled me to buy a violin. Mrs. George E. White, sensing evidences of talent in me, procured a violin teacher for me. Within a few months I had advanced as much as a sixth-year student, my teacher said. At the same time, eager to run my hands on a keyboard, I asked for a janitorial job in school, so that I might have the key to the auditorium, which housed the only piano in the campus.

I'd get out of the dormitory after midnight, walk over to the auditorium and practice on the piano, at least one hour each night. Another piano was at the Brewsters' house. Mrs. Brewster was kind enough to let me practice there whenever I had a chance to make the journey.

Soon I could play the hymns with both hands and four parts. When I was sixteen, I organized a quartet, then a sextet, then a forty-voice mixed choir. We were giving occasional recitals under my direction.

Quite often, on Sunday evenings, we had a chance to visit Dean Compton's home, where we listened to records of Caruso, Kreisler, and Heifetz. Concurrently, I realized how much I liked subjects related to science. Our teacher, Maurice Bigelow, would lecture to us, with a sense of humor, on physics, mathematics, and chemistry. Miss Anthony would explain to us the discoveries of Darwin and the experiments of Burbank.

The world of science was a totally different world from all the conflict and violence I had experienced previously. But there were glaring inconsistencies between our Christian faith and what these missionary teachers taught us.

I was confused. But nothing shattered my dreams more than the 1929 stock market crash. No, I had no investments. But those agencies that might have supported my musical education had now assumed a negative attitude.

Boldly I journeyed to Paris, France, to continue my musical education. But the economic impact of the stock market crash stopped my dreams and ambitions. It was more practical to come to the United States and study engineering. Uncle Hagop's seven daughters in Boston made such a project a reality.

I shall not speak of the nine years of depression and hardship into which I had just plunged. It is more important to discourse on what happened to my Christian faith.

*   *   *

Arthur S. Yeranian: What Happened Afterwards

In 1923, Arthur traveled to Thessaloniki, Greece, thanks to the help of his uncle, where he studied at Anatolia College preparatory school. While at Anatolia, he enjoyed the sciences, but loved music. This was a passion that would remain with him throughout his life.

Arthur S. Yeranian

The loveliness of Greece, however, was not to be the permanent home of Arthur. In 1930, young Arthur, born on George Washington's birthday, sailed on the S.S. George Washington to a new life with family in the United States. Upon arrival in his new homeland, Arthur lived initially with his cousin, Olympia Yeranian, in Boston.

The desire to succeed led Arthur to enroll at North Eastern

University. After five years of tedious work, he graduated as an electrical engineer and moved to Fresno, California. During the Second World War, Arthur worked as an electrical engineer for the United States government at a facility in San Bernardino, California.

The end of the war brought a new life to Arthur—married life. In 1945, Arthur married Rebecca Shamlian. This marriage was blessed for over 47 years, with companionship and a daughter, Lily, and five grandchildren.

In 1950, Arthur began to work for the Pacific Gas & Electric Company [PG&E] (the largest public utility in Northern California) as an electrical engineer. His 25 years with PG&E brought Arthur to the forefront as an engineer. His creativity and ingenuity are felt by many Californians every time they use an electrical appliance or turn on a light.

Some of Arthur's most lasting achievements in life occurred after his retirement in 1975. Coming out of retirement, he traveled at the request of several South American governments to their countries to develop their power distribution systems. In 1980, Arthur published his book *The Civilized*. This book was well received by both the Armenian and non-Armenian community. During his later years, Arthur had time to spend with his music. He was an accomplished pianist, violinist, and vocalist, as well as the composer of the symphonic piece titled "From the Hye-Land."

Arthur was listed in the Who's Who of California. He and Rebecca lived in Lafayette, California, for 27 years. His daughter, Lily, is the wife of Pastor Charles Kazarian, and the mother of five children. His half-brothers—Paul, Minas, and Sarkis Kullukian—all lived in the San Francisco Bay Area. In the early morning of Sunday, April 5, 1992, after a lengthy illness, Arthur left the physical trials of this life and went to sleep in the care of Jesus.

CHAPTER 10
HAGOP SHAMLIAN:
AN UNSUNG HERO OF MARASH

God's love is a safety net on life's slippery slope.
—Author Unknown

Hagop Shamlian (back row, center)

Hagop Shamlian was the eldest son born to Toros and Isgouhi Shamlian in Marash, Turkey in 1866. He attended school until the age of 16 and then entered the family trade of shoemaking. He worked with his father to support the family that included his mother, two sisters, and two brothers. Since the family owned land in the neighboring region of Bazarjik, Hagop was also involved in farming.

Soon after the massacre of 1896, Hagop's two brothers, Arsen and

Garabed, immigrated to Boston. Their departure left him, as the eldest son, to help his father, Toros, and support the family, but it also signaled the beginning of Hagop's and Toros' pioneering efforts as the single manufacturers of European-style leather in Marash.

Through their trade as shoemakers, Hagop and his father realized that the native method of tanning could only produce leather for slippers. On the other hand, the European method rendered the leather durable enough for the manufacture of sole and upper leather for shoes.

Hagop gathered as much information about tanning as he could by acquiring books on the European method from England and America. Initially, he and his father and mother did some experimental tanning at home in their underground bathhouse which had hot and cold water facilities. After a few smelly trials, they perfected their method and were eventually able to build their own tannery near Ghanledere, where they manufactured high-quality shoe leather. With increasing demand, the Shamlian leather was sold throughout Marash and the surrounding provinces and was also merchandised in Aleppo, Syria. In 1898, Hagop married Rebecca Kouyoumjian, a graduate of the Marash Girls' College, from the neighboring village of Hasan-Beyli. Their three children, Puzant, Helen, and Hrant, were born between the years of 1899 to 1903. In 1905, Rebecca died and, shortly afterwards, Hagop married Heranoush Nalbandian. Together they had six children: Evelyn, Toros, Rebecca, Edward, Isgouhi, and Arlene.

In his business and family dealings, Hagop based his life on Christian principles. Whatever extra money he had, he contributed for the affairs of the church. Although he had little formal education, he was hungry for knowledge and took every opportunity to attend lectures given by Armenian professors and American missionaries.

In 1915 and 1916, when the Armenians of Marash were deported and many to the Syrian desert, the Shamlian family living in the Sheikh-Mahallesi district was notified of deportation three different times. On the first two occasions, the orders were abruptly cancelled by the Turkish authorities. The third time, the Shamlians had all of their transportable belongings in front of their house, when suddenly

Hagop was called to the Turkish army base in the city. He was told that he and his family would not be deported. Instead, Hagop's tannery would cure leather needed by the Turkish army. In turn, the leather would be packaged and shipped to other factories that made items for the military.

The following is from an oral interview with Hagop's daughter, Rebecca Shamlian Yeranian, conducted in the Spring of 1988.

"Even before the war, Grandfather had both Turks and Armenians working in his factory. As a result of this commission (receiving permission by the Turks to produce leather in his tannery) he had to take on more workers which he did again from both groups among whom were Armenians, Avedis Soghomonian, Aram Mississian and Aram Poladian. He also did something else. He was asked by parents of wealthy young Armenian and Turkish boys to have the government issue exemption cards so that the young men wouldn't have to go into the army and would instead work in his tannery. He went to the authorities and permission was granted. What happened was this: these boys who knew nothing about tanning would report to Hagop's tannery in the early hours of the morning, show their exemption cards, stay for a while and then leave and go about their business. At least two hundred or more boys were saved in this way from serving in the army.

During the war, Hagop would invite German missionaries to his home along with Armenian couples. He would be asked by these Armenian parents to intercede on behalf of their sons when they were thrown into Turkish prisons. He did this and managed to get a number of boys out of prison by telling the Turkish officials that the boys in prison "weren't doing them any good. They'd be better off out of prison and working." He was respected by the Turkish leaders of the city and trusted by them as he was an honest man and so they followed through on his advice."

During the short period of peace between WWI and the rise of Ataturk, Hagop again showed his willingness to rebuild the Armenian community in Marash. As the Armenians returned to their homes from the deportation, the people of each quarter made plans to reestablish their churches and schools. The Armenian community of the First Congregational Church was able to retrieve the three steeple bells that the Turks had taken away to melt for ammunition. Under the supervision of Tahktaji Hagop Chilingirian, Hagop's second cousin, the Armenians gathered at the foot of the church bell tower to bid for the honor of ringing the bells, once again, to raise money for the most-needy refugees. After half an hour of bidding, Hagop placed the highest bid of 44 Turkish gold pieces, and his eldest son, Puzant, was chosen to ring the bells for the first time since the war.

Hagop also worked diligently to help Armenian families reestablish themselves in Marash. Among his humanitarian efforts was the financing of a general store in Marash for two brothers, his wife's nephews, whose resources were limited.

In 1920, as the Turkish revolution intensified, Hagop left his family in the care of the American missionaries and with thousands of Armenians, fled Marash with the French forces. Finally, he arrived in Beirut where his eldest son, Puzant, was studying tanning chemistry at the American University. Because the Armenian community in Marash was nearly obliterated by the massacres, it was decided that Puzant should go to America in the hope of moving the family there.

In July of 1920, Puzant left Beirut with Karnig Babigian, Ghevont Chorbajian, and Toros Shamlian (a cousin), all of Marash. By ship, they traveled to Marseilles and then to New York.

Puzant eventually settled in San Francisco. In 1939, through the efforts of his aunt, Ferideh Shamlian Vagim, he began the process of resettling the entire family in California. By 1941, the entire family came to reside in America.

Finally, Hagop Shamlian became a citizen of the United States. He died in 1960 at the age of 94.

CHAPTER 11
PUZANT SHAMLIAN:
A BIOGRAPHY

If opportunity doesn't knock, build a door.
—Milton Berle

Puzant Shamlian (fourth from left)

Puzant Shamlian's recollections about his father, Hagop Shamlian, were completed on December 20, 1980 and transcribed by his daughter, Margaret Elaine Shamlian. The following biography was written by Margaret Elaine Shamlian, daughter of Puzant Shamlian, and has been edited with additional comments by Ellen Sarkisian Chesnut, the author of this book:

Knowing that the situation for Armenians in Turkey was growing worse by the day, Hagop Shamlian decided that his eldest son should go to America and work to transplant the rest of the family out of Turkey and to the United States.

The family's relatives in Boston had heard of the Marash massacres and fearing the rest of the family dead, had sent $350 ship fare to Puzant through the Near East Relief agency. Mr. Charles Perrine, the American teacher, lent him an additional $50 needed for the total fare. So it was, that after only one year at S.P.C. (aka Syrian Protestant College), on July 7, 1920, Puzant boarded a French ship named "Lotus" in Beirut and sailed to America.

As an Armenian, he was a refugee from persecution of the most abhorrent nature. He was willing to work at anything to get his family away from the atrocities of the Turks. When he arrived in America he had no money. Although his cousin in Boston had sponsored his immigration, he stayed there only a short time. After a few days his uncles in California sent him the train fare so that he could travel to the West Coast. Like most Armenians, he arrived in California because he had a few relatives in the state. He knew nothing of the "pot of gold" said to be in California.

Puzant and the majority of the Armenians who arrived in California in the 1920s did not come to capture a dream but to build through their own efforts a better existence than the one Turkey had offered.

Perhaps it is a coincidence that many Armenians settled in and around Fresno. It had a dry climate similar to that of the Armenian Plateau in Turkey. Generally, the pioneers of the Armenian colony in Fresno spent years in Armenian colonies in the industrial centers of the East Coast. Sooner or later these people wanted to leave factory life and were attracted by the favorable climate and good opportunities in the West. The desire to own land, of which there seemed plenty in California, was the motivation for the establishment of an Armenian center in this state.

By the time Puzant arrived here the Armenian community in Fresno had been established for about 25 years. In 1920s, there were more than 4,000 Armenians in and around Fresno. Although they were hardworking and quick to establish themselves in business or as farmers, their mere numbers resulted in a resentful attitude on the part of the native white residents in the area. The Armenians were culturally very different from both the native white Americans and the immigrants born in Northern and Western Europe. The fact and extent of this cultural difference shaped much of their experience in the United States and especially in California.

The resentment towards the Armenians was manifested in their being prohibited from buying land in certain neighborhoods in Fresno. Also, in the Protestant churches of Fresno, sections in the back of the church were set aside for Armenians. Just as the Asians and Blacks were given offensive titles, the Armenians were referred to as the "Fresno Indians" and as the "inches" as they asked in Armenian, *inch*?, which means why or what.

It took the Armenians years of hard work and dedication as good citizens to dispel the resentment and prejudice that encompassed their Fresno environment.

Puzant's first home in California was in the agricultural community of Yettem near Fresno. As soon as he arrived he began to work as a laborer on the farms of his uncles, as well as on the neighboring farms. He also worked on the highway that was being built between Yettem and the Sierra Nevadas. At this time, these were the only jobs open to Armenians, unless they were able to start a private business. The local white businessmen posted signs in their shop windows reading "Armenians need not apply."

Luckily for Puzant, he spent only a year and a half in Yettem. It happened that a friend of his was driving to San Francisco for a vacation and Puzant decided to go along for the ride. His desire to visit the museums and art galleries of the city, as well as to attend night school, influenced his decision to stay in San Francisco and look for a job. Because he had learned English while attending Syrian Protestant College, he was not hampered by a language problem as were many newly arrived immigrants. However, he still attended night school to improve his English and wrote letters to Mr. Perrine so that his former teacher could correct his grammar and send the letters back.

As a fully experienced tanner, he easily found a job at the

Eagle Tannery at San Bruno Avenue and Army Street. (Army Street is now called Cesar Chavez Street.) After about a year and a half, he was offered a skilled buffer's job at a competing tannery. His youth and skill as a buffer were the cause of a great deal of jealousy on the part of an older employee, who had wanted Puzant's job. This made working conditions very difficult. Finally, he quit the tannery after the older employee called him a "Damn Armenian" and tried to beat him up. Being the younger, Puzant easily stopped his attacks, but the mental strain of working in the tannery and his worrying about the desperate conditions of his family in Marash had destroyed his desire to live.

Despondent and out of work, he often visited a friend who worked at the Caldow Paint Company on Market Street. On one of these visits, the owner, Mr. Caldow, asked him if he could paint and repair the house of a customer who lived in Ross. Although he had never done any painting before, he immediately agreed to take the job.

For six weeks he painted, wallpapered, and repaired the house in Ross. He was paid $156 for the job. No sooner had he received the money than he got a letter from his father. Hagop Shamlian needed $150 to get the family out of Marash to safer quarters in Aleppo, Syria. Puzant immediately sent the money and was relieved that his family had finally left Turkey.

At the end of the six weeks, Mr. Caldow came to inspect Puzant's work on the house in Ross. He was amazed at the natural affinity he showed for this type of work. The job was finished on Friday afternoon and by Friday evening Mr. Caldow had hired Puzant as one of his paint clerks.

His association with Caldow Paint Company lasted 14 years. After eight years as a clerk, he became an outside salesman and would travel down the Peninsula, as far as Sunnyvale. He figured his living expenses carefully in order to send most of each paycheck to his family.

It was as an employee at Caldow Paint that he realized his desire to become an artist. The well-known California landscape artist, George Demont Otis, did business with Mr. Caldow. Since he had a studio, Puzant asked him if he might give him lessons in drawing and painting. The first twelve lessons were in pencil drawing only, and as the lessons progressed Mr. Otis encouraged Puzant to take up dry point etching as well as painting. Aside from the in-class drawing sessions, part of the course was conducted on Sundays. Mr. Otis and Puzant would drive around Marin County or down the coast to Pedro Point to sketch landscapes which were finished in oil at home. The noted California colorist, R. Jerome Jones, also contributed to Puzant's studies as an artist.

Although his job at Caldow Paint was steady work, Puzant felt that it was a dead end. He wanted to someday manufacture paint under his own label, and he wasn't learning the important aspects of the paint business from Mr. Caldow.

Finally, in 1937, he decided to borrow on the cash value of a life insurance policy he had unwillingly acquired. With $1,256, he rented a store on Gough Street and started his own Bay City Paint Company. He couldn't afford the $50 a month rent so he shared the store with a friend who was an engraver who set up his press in the back and paid one-third of the rent. While Puzant went out to solicit business from house painters and auto repair shops, his friend minded the store.

While operating his store on Gough Street, he developed his own line of artist oil colors, which he put in tubes by hand. Though his store hours were 8 a.m. to 6 p.m. Monday through Saturday, he often worked until midnight doing the partial bookkeeping and filling cans with paints and thinners.

After he had been in business for one year, he felt he could start to bring his family to America. It was now 1938 and he had to sponsor a total of 12 relatives. His family had saved enough money for the total ship fare, and he didn't have to send them additional funds for their passage. However, he did have to file affidavits of good credit with Dun Bradstreet and the Bank of America in order for his relatives to be granted visas. After the necessary papers were filed, his father and step-mother arrived in California in 1938. By 1941, the entire family resided in San Francisco.

Puzant's business was also growing during this time. By 1940, he realized that he needed larger quarters for his expanding inventory. He purchased a larger building on Market Street in the Eureka Valley district. In 1941 he moved his business and 2279 Market Street became the new home of the Bay City Paint Company.

Through the years, the Bay City Paint Company became one of the foremost suppliers of household, industrial, and artist paint materials on the West Coast. The orders for Puzant's refinishing products come from as far away as Salt Lake City and Mexico. His "Byzantine Standard" artist colors were shipped as far as Barcelona, Spain and French Polynesia. The most unique facet of his business was his specialty of matching colors by eye. When given a color sample which is not a stock color, he combined his practical knowledge of paint chemistry, as well as his artist's eye for color, and could match "any color to any type finish." For example, artificial limb manufacturers sent their customers to him and he matched the artificial limb exactly to the person's skin tone. His talent as a color specialist became part of his business for 50 years and benefitted homeowners and interior decorators, as well as refinishers and industrial designers.

Charles Chaves, professor in the Fine Arts Department at Laney College in Oakland, California, remembers buying gallons of oil paints while a student at the San Francisco Art Institute from Puzant at Bay City Paint Company.

If we look at the scope of Puzant Shamlian's business and personal endeavors the underlying quality in his life is that he was a contributor. First, he looked beyond himself and was willing to contribute to the well-being of his family. Second, he readily experimented with paints and coatings to improve his business. Last, he spent many hours studying form and color to transfer the California landscapes he loved on to canvas and dry point etching on copper. In short, the dream that California held for him was not in the "place" we know as California. The dream of prosperity was within himself. He drew upon his own resourcefulness to achieve what to him was a prosperous and happy life.

In 1944, Puzant met Viola Bakalian at a dinner at the Bethany Armenian Congregational Church in Oakland, California. It took him one year to get up the courage to ask her for a date. When he finally did, Viola's father exclaimed in

Armenian, "This one will never do; he's too slow." Puzant made up for lost time by asking Viola to marry him on the first date. She said, "I can't marry you, I don't even know you!" They continued to see each other and after a year's courtship, they married on July 24, 1946. Initially they lived in the flat above Puzant's paint store. Their son, James Puzant was born on September 22, 1947. Their daughter, Margaret Elaine was born on March 19, 1949. In 1951, they bought a home and moved to 1815 15th Avenue in San Francisco. Their third child, Phillip Hrant, was born on January 18, 1954.

CHAPTER 12
HELEN SHAMLIAN DAVID AND HER BROTHER, HRANT SHAMLIAN

Helen Shamlian (back row, fourth from left) Alleppo, 1923

H elen Shamlian David and her brother, Hrant Shamlian, were the younger siblings of Puzant. Their father was Hagop Shamlian and their mother was Hagop's first wife, Rebecca Kouyoumjian, who was born in 1873 in Hasan Beyli, Turkey, and died in 1905. Helen was born in Marash on June 30, 1901, and her brother, Hrant, was born on October 2, 1903.

Neither Helen nor her brother, Hrant, experienced deportation or massacre, but both were victims nevertheless. They lived in the toxic environment of Ottoman Turkey inundated by ever more horrendous news of one bloodbath after another—Armenians being tortured, burned alive, raped, and killed—perpetrated by either Turks or Kurds and often times both acting in collusion. Is it any wonder that this would exact a toll on the most vulnerable?

Hrant, Aleppo, Syria 1920s

Helen was a beautiful girl and grew to be an even more beautiful young woman. She suffered a nervous breakdown in January 1920 at the onset of the Battle of Marash terrified that she would be kidnapped and raped by Turks or Kurds. Her mental illness caused her to alienate herself from her family. Her stepsisters, Evelyn and Rebecca, experienced her strange behavior when they were students at the primary school in Syria and she was one of the teachers: Helen acted as if she didn't even know them. At that time also she was being fawned over by fellow female teachers who kept telling her how beautiful she was. At home, she began to treat Heranoush, her stepmother, as if she was a servant and was extremely disrespectful to her.

Helen left Syria before 1930 and came to America. She married an Armenian by the name of Dicran David on April 14, 1933. He was a soldier in the First World War and had been subjected to nerve gas on the front lines. He suffered terribly from respiratory problems. There is no record as to when he died. Following his death, she was searching for some kind of solace and joined the "Church" of Aimee Semple McPherson.

All of the Shamlians, including my mother and father, were now living in San Francisco. Helen would frequently visit our flat on Seventeenth Street. Everything seemed to be going well until one afternoon when she had an outburst and began to verbally attack my mother. We children heard the commotion and literally drove her out of the house. Even with her unpredictable behavior, she was invited to my Aunt Rebecca's wedding to Arthur Yeranian. This was in the 1940s. Helen yelled out something profane during the marriage ceremony.

She lived alone in one of her Edwardian flats on Castro Street. When I was walking nearby, I would frequently see her looking out of one of the living room windows. Her beauty was long gone and her features coarsened with the passing of the years and her mental distress.

When she died, her brother let her siblings into her flat to help themselves to what was left of her furniture and belongings.

My mother and I visited her when she was still alive. Her flat was neat and tidy. I remember a large doll with a porcelain face and enormous eyes draped over a chair wearing maroon velvet finery. It was a beautiful doll but not one that I would want to hold.

Helen died on August 29, 1967. I don't even remember if there was a church service for her. A sad life and a sad end.

Her brother Hrant was a lively boy and very bright. One episode on the streets of Marash would change his life forever. He was playing out in front of the house when he saw a mortally wounded male Kurd staggering down the street covered in blood. Hrant became so distraught that he ended up getting sick so that his parents put him to bed. Whereupon, he began developing an extremely high fever, so high that he lost consciousness. After a week in this condition, he miraculously woke up. The result was that he was forever afflicted by epilepsy. Heranoush, his stepmother, cared for him lovingly and unselfishly throughout his life. He wanted so much to attend school with the rest of his siblings and would have excelled as he was very smart but that was not an option with his seizures. He died in Iraq in the 1930s after having a seizure at the top of stone steps whereupon he tumbled to his death.

REST IN PEACE HELEN AND HRANT.

CHAPTER 13
HERANOUSH NALBANDIAN SHAMLIAN

There is no charm equal to tenderness of heart
—Jane Austin

Heranoush Nalbandian Shamlian

Heranoush Nalbandian Shamlian was born in Kilis, Turkey (Ottoman Empire); and, according to pages removed from a very old family bible, the date of her birth was January 12, 1882. She was the youngest child of Hagop Nalbandian, who was born on July 31, 1837. Hagop was the eldest of five siblings:

Hagop	b. July 31, 1837
Miriam	b. February 1845
Grigor	b. May 15, 1850
Ovhannes	b. December 1851
Sultan	b. April 10, 1861

Hagop subsequently had five children. Nowhere on the pages removed from the family bible is the name of the mother of Hagop and his siblings or the name of the mother of Hagop's children:

Rahael	b. December 27, 1866
Miriam	b. May 10, 1872
Vahan	b. January 24, 1875
Shamiram	b. July 24, 1878
Heranoush	b. January 12, 1882

Heranoush told the story, in later years, of how her parents, after her birth, put her in a corner hoping she would die. Girls were thought, in some Armenian communities, to be burdens on their families. She also recounted that as an infant, in that same corner, she showed such a tremendous will to live that her parents decided that they would let her survive and started caring for her.

That magnanimous gesture did not, however, transfer into Heranoush getting an education. She was not allowed to go to school and was instead taught the necessary skills of cooking and sewing. She became very accomplished in both areas.

Hagop Shamlian, a native of Marash, was widowed with three young children. Somehow he learned about Heranoush and visited her parents to ask for her hand in marriage. He was sixteen years older than her and was considered to be a good prospect for a husband as he was very hardworking and had a solid trade as a tanner.

Heranoush was more than anxious to see what he looked like and saw him as she was hanging laundry and nearly strangled herself on the clothesline as she thought he was the handsomest man she had ever seen.

They married and besides caring for her stepchildren—Puzant, Helen and Hrant—she had six children herself with Hagop: Toros,

Evelyn, Rebecca, Edward, and Isgouhi, and in 1925, another child also named Isgouhi Arlene.

Her fool-hearty behavior and bravery during the aftermath of the Battle of Marash were legendary to her family.

It was not easy in the 1920s, living in Syria as refugees from Marash after the flush days of life in Turkey. Heranoush had to literally make bread out of stone as there was so little money coming in. Evelyn and Rebecca remembered going to school with no lunch (after a very basic breakfast) but they pretended near their classmates that they had already eaten as they played together in the schoolyard.

Circumstances were better for the family when they moved to Iraq in the 1930s. However, living in such a conservative Muslim country was not easy for Christians. With the sponsorship of Hagop's eldest son, Puzant, and Hagop's sister, Ferideh, Hagop and Heranoush were the first of the Shamlian family to leave the Middle East for America in 1938.

They lived first in the building owned by their son Puzant at 16th and Market streets. It was a very old two-story Victorian with a large yard that encircled the property. After that, I remember the small apartment they resided in located on Castro Street across from Market Street.

Physically, Heranoush was a small woman with large expressive brown eyes and a prominent chin. She would twist her long, beautiful silvery gray braid around her finger and make a tight bun. She had a small tattoo inside her wrist of an anchor and a cross put there by an itinerant tattooist in Kilis when she was a girl.

Sometime in the early 1950s, my mother got her enrolled in a class at Sanchez Elementary School, one block from our house on Seventeenth Street. The purpose of her being there was to learn English so she would be able to take the test to become a citizen of the United States. I remember she introduced me to her new friend, an Italian woman, who was also there to learn.

But her crowning achievement was in the summer class in the Armenian language. It was held at St. John's Armenian Church when it was located on Pearl Street off of Market. She was determined to learn to read and write in Armenian. Mrs. Parensem Paul was our language teacher. My grandmother was the star pupil of the class. I wrote a haiku years later commemorating her achievement:

Key to alphabet
took her sixty years to find
her letters are blest.

When my grandmother suffered a heart attack, my mother rushed to the hospital where she was being cared for. She was with her for hours and hated to leave her but she had a family to look after.

A day or so later, the hospital phoned and told my mother, Heranoush, had died. This was February 16, 1956. My aunt, Rebecca, and my mother, Evelyn, were inconsolable thinking of their beautiful mother, her sacrifices for her family, her talents, her big heart, and her mischievous sense of humor.

It was an honor to have known her even though it was for such a short time in my life.

CHAPTER 14

TESTIMONY OF TOROS SHAMLIAN

The mind is not a vessel to be filled, but a fire to be kindled.
— Plutarch

Rebecca (left), Toros (center), and Evelyn (right)

Toros Shamlian was born on August 12, 1906 and died in San Mateo, California, on August 16, 1997. The following testimony of Toros Shamlian was shared on January 18, 1988, through an oral interview with his niece, Ellen Sarkisian Chesnut, in San Mateo, California:

We lived in a two-story house in the Sheikh-Mahallesi quarter along with many other Armenian families. Our second floor was not yet finished. The basement contained a bath that was built when my grandfather, Toros, was alive. I remember carpets rolled up that my father, Hagop, had purchased from the German principal of the Beth Shalom Orphanage.

I studied at the Beth Shalom (or Beytchallum) School for four years. There were a few children like myself who did not live at the orphanage. My sister, Evelyn, attended the First Evangelical School. Even though there were only Armenian teachers in these schools, we were forbidden to use our Armenian language. Only the Turkish and German languages were allowed at Beth Shalom. At home, we even spoke Turkish.

My father, Hagop, owned a large tannery. My older half-brother, Puzant, worked for him and I did my part by carrying food from home to the tannery for my father and brother. In 1915 and 1916, when the Armenians of Marash were being deported, my father hired fifty to sixty Armenian men as workers in the tannery, thus saving them from being deported.

Because he made such high-quality leather, the government did not deport him or our immediate family. Instead, the leather from his tannery was used to make boots and other items for the Ottoman army.

As a young man, my father was a member of the Social Democrat, Hunchak, a political party. We lived in dangerous times. He claimed there were at least six times when he came very close to death but miraculously survived.

Here is a story of one of those times, in my father's own words: "The town of Zeitoun was close to Marash. The Zeitounzis, being highlanders, loved their freedom and were a gigantic thorn in the side of the repressive Ottoman government. The Zeitounzis needed weapons and gunpowder with which to defend themselves. A friend and I decided to help by delivering gunpowder. One night after our donkeys were loaded down with saddlebags filled with gunpowder, we started for Zeitoun. All of a sudden, in the distance, we saw on horseback two Turkish gendarmes heading our way. Luckily for us, we were close to the Armenian cemetery so we abandoned our pack animals and made a run for it. We hid behind some tombstones. Then, seemingly out of nowhere, a powerful wind swept through the area. We saw that the gendarmes, with difficulty, moved toward Marash. We remained where we were for another half hour. When we got back to the donkeys, the flaps on the saddlebags had been flung loose and the gunpowder had blown away. We did not continue toward Zeitoun but, instead, went to my aunt's home close by and remained there till morning." Here ends my father's recollections.

Toros continued with his recollections:

I remember clearly the day the Battle of Marash started. My eldest half-brother, Puzant, was in Beirut at the American University (prior to 1920s known as Syrian Protestant College), studying tanning chemistry. My mother, Heranoush, was preparing dough for lavash. My young friend, Budik, and I were to take this dough to the German orphanage for baking. After we arrived, we waited for the bread to be baked. I noticed a French soldier looking through his binoculars at Mt. Akhur, aka Akhur Dagh. The soldier spoke aloud, saying "There's going to be fighting today!"

When the bread was done, Budik and I hurriedly left—Budik to his house and I to mine. I burst into the kitchen and loudly exclaimed to my mother, "There's going to be a battle today!" She was busy with kitchen chores and told me to go away. While I continued pestering my mother about the battle, my two cousins, Dicran and Haroutune (who were sons of my mother's sister, Shamiram and her husband, Abraham Berberian) dropped by. They were on their way back to their home from the store, where they worked. They told us that an old man saw them and angrily asked, "What are you doing here? Can't you see all the stores are closed and everybody's gone home? Go! Close the store and go home!" They left.

My mother insisted that my cousins stay while she

prepared something for them to eat. I could hardly wait to tell them what the French soldier had said. My mother chimed in, "What battle?" I replied, "You'll see in a little while." Then, I took my rope and went out to the yard to play. A few minutes later, we all heard a cannon shot. I ran into the house and yelled out gleefully, "Didn't I tell you the battle would start!"

My mother told her nephews there was no way they could go home. They would have to stay with us. Dicran and Haroutune's home was in the quarter of Marash populated by Turks.

"What would happen to their family?" we wondered aloud. Then my father came home from the tannery. An Armenian legionnaire by the name of Sarkis Chavush arrived to look after our neighborhood. He became our leader. We had five rifles with which to protect our entire group.

At night, Sarkis Chavush snuck out and went over to where the Turkish mosque was located. Upon returning, he said the mosque was filled to capacity with Turks who had fled their homes for the safety of the mosque, as their homes were being fired upon by the French. Sarkis Chavush had our neighbors stand guard and take turns at their positions. Sadly, we were running out of food and supplies. After ten days of holding out, Sarkis Chavush and our male neighbors decided that all of us: men, women, children, and old folks would have to make a run for the safe haven of the Latin Monastery. Sarkis Chavush assigned the carrying of sacks of food to the children. I was given a sack. Luckily for us, other Armenian legionnaires arrived to lead us to safety. Now, almost the entire population of the neighborhood gathered in front of our house. We would disperse in small groups. My sister, Evelyn, was in the group that followed a newly arrived Armenian legionnaire. She recalled later that they went through narrow passageways between homes, down alleyways—always moving quickly and quietly. Some of the Armenians in outlying quarters were too far away from us and were killed by the Turks. Only one man escaped the carnage and told us about it later.

I was with another boy when we made a run for the monastery. We followed the stream near my father's tannery. From there we climbed up to the monastery. Rooms were made available for the Armenians who had escaped. My family—my mother Heranoush, brothers Hrant and Edward, sisters Evelyn, Rebecca, and Isgouhi, and myself—remained at the monastery for five days.

At this time, French soldiers were coming under increasing attack in other regions of southeastern Turkey, as well. Unbeknownst to the Armenians, the French were planning to leave. On February 10, we saw a French plane that had flown to Marash from Adana. Leaflets were dropped from the plane, ordering French soldiers to leave Marash for Adana. We Armenians were gripped by panic when we realized we were being abandoned. My father knew that if he remained in Marash, he was a dead man. (Turks had already warned him.) He decided to leave with the French. But where was he? Then, I heard his voice outside the monastery. Our entire family rushed to his side. He kissed all of us goodbye. It could not have been worse for the French soldiers and the 3,000 Armenians who followed them. They went into one of the worst blizzards in memory. Snowstorms ranged round the mountains and gorges.

Meanwhile, our family decided to leave the monastery and go to another safe space for refuge. Helen was already there at the Marash Girls' College. As soon as I could, I left the monastery with two men, one of whom said he knew where the college was located. We ended up going around in circles.

Finally, someone came along who knew the way. Even though it was snowing and freezing cold, we found the college. I was in the first group who made it. My family and others arrived shortly after. The whole group congregated in a very large room. We remained at the college for two weeks. When a cease fire was called, we left the college and found refuge at another safe haven, Garabed Agha Bilesjekjian's house. While there, our youngest sister, Isgouhi, died from a measles epidemic along with five other children. She was a blond, blue-eyed beautiful child, and smart too. It was a heart-breaking loss for us. So when another girl was born in 1925, my mother named her, her last child, Isgouhi Arlene.

Meanwhile, as we found out later, our father almost lost his feet from frostbite on the trek but, fortunately, a doctor removed some of his frostbitten toes instead. After his hospital stay in Adana, he went to Beirut, where Puzant, my half-brother, was studying. Someone told my brother that a man in tattered clothing was asking for him. When Puzant went outside, he discovered with profound happiness—it was his father.

Hagop left Beirut and went to Aleppo, where he found work as a tanner. He began to send money to us from Aleppo but none reached us.

My mother's money ran out. Mother decided then and there, "If I'm going to die, I'd like to die under my own roof. C'mon children, we're going home!"

My mother received permission from the Turkish authorities to go back to our house. Helen remained at the Marash Girls' College.

It was nighttime when we returned. It looked as if nobody lived there. We tiptoed up to the second floor. There were six of us returning: my mother Heranoush, sisters Evelyn and Rebecca, half-brother Hrant, younger brother Edward, and myself. We had comforters with us.

The next morning, we were confronted by the Turk Ahmet who had taken over our home. He began screaming at us. My mother calmly told him to speak with an imam about the situation. So Ahmet did. The imam said that it was our home after all. So we were able to remain. We lived with the Turk, his wife, and in-laws. At that time, my mother needed help financially. So, I had to learn a trade to earn some money.

There was a weaving conglomerate in the home next to the Bilesjekjian house. It was there in the basement that four looms were set up. Three weavers were working and they put me to work on the fourth loom. A goat lived in the basement alongside the weavers. I remember weaving a small six-inch piece. However, I hated weaving.

It was on the day after two weeks at the loom, when my mother had returned from the market, that I told her I was not going to work there any longer. She knew how I longed to go back to school and she let me quit.

Now I joined my sisters, Evelyn and Rebecca, at the Armenian Orthodox Church School. Hrant couldn't go, as he was an epileptic and experienced grand mal seizures.

We did have some carefree moments after the Battle of Marash. One day, I decided to entertain Rebecca and Edward because they were crying I told Evelyn to hide underneath the comforter, as I was going to fool them into thinking she was not there. Then I called to her as if I was a magician: "Evelyn, come over here!" Just as she threw off the covers, a mouse rushed across the room from underneath the bed. Uproarious pandemonium ensued!

When Mustafa Kemal advised Armenians to leave Turkey, we did just that in 1921. We were going to Aleppo, Syria.

The life of Toros Shamlian beyond the Battle of Marash is further inspirational and was written by his eldest daughter, Dr. Linda Shamlian Force in 1997 as follows:

Toros Hagop Shamlian was born in Marash, Turkey, on August 12, 1906. His father, Hagop Shamlian, had three children with his first wife, Rebecca Kouyoumjian Shamlian, who passed away. His second wife, Heranoush Nalbandian Shamlian, was Toros' mother. Toros was the eldest of six siblings, which included Evelyn, Rebecca, Edward, and Isgouhi and, in 1925, Arlene. Rebecca had a twin, a boy, who passed away at childbirth. Toros' half brothers and sister were Puzant Shamlian, Helen Shamlian David, and Hrant Shamlian. This latter child suffered from epilepsy and passed away as an adult in the 1930s.

Toros' parents, fearing an attack by the Turks, changed Toros' birth year to 1907. Their thinking was that, if he were younger, this would reduce his chances of being killed. The memory of the devastation wrought by the Hamidian Massacres of 1894-1896 was ever present. Toros was a very active boy, exploring Marash with either his sister Evelyn or his other friends. Sadly, when he was twelve, he contracted polio. One of his legs was permanently and adversely affected. The leg muscles had atrophied. As a result, he had a permanent limp on his right leg. But this did not stop him. In his later years, he took up power walking and jogging. As a boy, Toros loved to read and his favorite subject was geometry. He taught himself mathematics, including algebra and trigonometry. This would serve him well when he entered college. Considering Toros was the first son, and considering his affinity for math and science, he was admitted to the American University of Beirut to study mechanical engineering and geophysics. He graduated in 1929. In the mid-1930s, he was offered a job as a geophysicist with the British Oil Development Company based in Iraq. In later years, this company was renamed British Petroleum [BP] and many BP gas stations are in the U.S. today.

In researching the history of Armenians, it was learned that, as far back as 7,000 years ago, Armenians were at the forefront as skilled mathematicians, architects, and craftsmen. Further, geometry has always held a very special interest to Armenians. This love of geometrical shapes and symbols supported the Armenian culture. As Toros' daughter, convinced that his DNA was programmed for a love of mathematics. I also believe that I have inherited my father's DNA as I have spent virtually my entire adult life being obsessed with mathematics and geometry.

My father married Arpine Adrouny on November 22, 1937. She was just 17 and her mother insisted she finish high school before marrying. My father was considerably older at 30 years of age. They were living in Iraq at the British compound. Two years later, a daughter was still born. Her name was Cynthia. In August 1941, the family immigrated to the United States and settled in San Francisco. Toros did not have any trouble finding work since he was a skilled engineer. At one point, he spent two to three years working in Sausalito, designing the Liberty Ships. His best friend was another engineer, Ed Meadows. After the war, the two applied for design engineers positions at Bechtel Corporation at 62 First Street in San Francisco. Dad was a project leader on numerous projects that included copper mines in South Africa and power plants in the U.S. He had a talent for teaching junior engineers how to design and took pleasure mentoring them. Infinitely loyal, he spent 32 years with the company and was very proud of the gold watch and special recognition they gave him upon his retirement.

I was born in 1942 and a younger sister Brenda was born 1945. My earliest recollections about my father date back to when I was two years old. Even at the early age, and continuing throughout my life, my father and I had a very special relationship. It actually went beyond "special." It was a recognition analogous to soul mates. Throughout my life, Dad and I seemed to be able to communicate through non-verbal means. This does not mean we did not speak to one another. We did… and quite prolifically. Rather, he and I would exchange looks and read each other's minds. This went on to the end, and even when I last saw him during Thanksgiving of 1996, and he was doing so poorly and could not speak, there were moments when he still got that special look in his eyes. AND THAT LOOK WAS LOVE.

My mother used to tease me by saying that Dad wanted a son, but he got a daughter instead. I guess with the special bonding between us it was natural and it prompted him to teach me many things. He taught me about life and he taught me about science and mathematics. With all this, though, he had a wonderful sense of play.

Toros taught me about his heritage and had many amusing anecdotes about his years at the American University of Beirut. I was totally shocked when he admitted that he and his friends would duck out and go sit at the top of a hill behind the university and smoke hashish. WOW… that really "blew my mind!"

And he liked me to help him build things in the garage and help him fix the car. I am sure I inherited his engineering genes. I can recall countless times when he would call me to help him with "Linda… hoss yegour meg vargan." This was Armenian for "come here for a minute." The one minute generally led to one hour, but I did not mind. I loved spending time with my father. I can recall being 18 years old and studying integral calculus I was really stuck on a homework problem and went down to the garage to ask him if he could make any sense out of it. What totally amazed me was that he spent 30 seconds reading the problem and answered, "That's easy." He then proceeded to outline the steps I needed to take to solve the problem. What amazed me was that he had been out of college for 30 years, and 30 years away from doing calculus… and yet, he could quickly assimilate and solve highly technical problems. I was totally thoroughly impressed by his intelligence in science. I am convinced he was a savant. I recall so clearly his taking me to Dietz Drafting Supplies store in downtown San Francisco. He bought me a very expensive slide rule (precursor to hand calculators of the 1970s). I still have it to this day. I also have his set of drafting instruments which he used in college and later in practice. I had a copy of one of his drawings of a cross section through a metal part. Standard nomenclature would be a series of slanted parallel lines indicating the view was a cross-section. I was totally amazed at the precision of doing this by hand in the 1920s... it was so exact that it looked like a computer-generated drawing! Even when I went back to school to get my structural engineering degree in the mid-1970s, Dad was very interested in the classes I was taking. I remember us talking about fluid dynamics and thermodynamics. We talked about physics and systems analysis. We talked about everything and anything dealing with engineering, science, and mathematics. I know he thoroughly enjoyed looking at my textbooks. Toros had many interests aside from science and mathematics. For example, he absolutely loved wrestling and made me sit with him watching the matches on the TV. He took me to live wrestling competitions at the Cow Palace in San Francisco. He was also crazy about horror movies. Every Saturday afternoon, the two of us would watch Caravan of Crime. I recall being 10 years old and he took me to the movies to see "House of Wax." I was so scared I had my head down during most of the film. Toros was a self-taught expert furniture builder. I still have the desk and bookshelves he made for me when I entered high school.

When I was four, Dad told me we were going to visit Uncle Puzant and Auntie Viola at Grandpa's house. It was a lazy Saturday afternoon, and one of those special cloudless days in San Francisco where the sky is a brilliant blue. I recall him holding my hand as we walked down 14th Street up to Market Street. I can recall us talking about different things like wild flowers growing in the empty lots we passed and the bees buzzing around us. It was always that way between the two of us. We were always able to communicate.

On that particular day, Uncle Sarkis (his sister Evelyn's

husband) and Uncle Edd e were visiting with Uncle Puzant. Grandma, Auntie Evelyn, and Auntie Viola were in the kitchen. What struck my young mind, and what I can still visualize to this day, were the close bonds, esteem, and affection among the three brothers and Uncle Sarkis, and the pleasant (although sometimes highly energetic) conversation as the afternoon drifted into sunset. I remember all telling funny and colorful jokes in Turkish so that cousin Ellen (daughter of Uncle Sarkis and Auntie Evelyn) and I would not be able to understand what they were talking about. If something went wrong, he would curse in Turkish. To this day, I occasiona ly have a Turkish cuss word pop out, emulating my father. I also remember my father walking me to visit Auntie Ruby and Uncle Arthur in their flat on Castro Street. And I remember how happy he was when Uncle Eddie got engaged to Auntie Roxie. I also remember how much he enjoyed visiting with Auntie Arlene and her husband, Uncle Dick.

Dad loved all of his family. He was the quintessential father and had an infinite capacity for patience, understanding, and caring. He was the sweetest man that I have ever known and did not have a mean bone in his body. He was kind to everyone. He was honest and had integrity in everything he did. He was also the smartest engineer I ever met. I followed in his footsteps and in 40 years never met an engineer that could hold a candle to him. To this day, he is in my heart and receives my utmost respect and love.

CHAPTER 15
RECOLLECTIONS OF
EVELYN SHAMLIAN SARKISIAN

The important thing is this:
To be able at any moment, to sacrifice what we are
for what we could become.
—*Maharishi MaheshYogi*

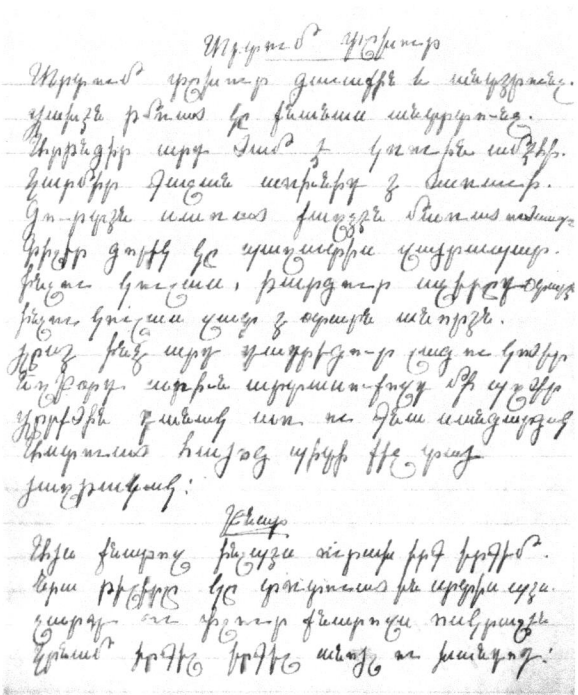

Sample of Evelyn's writing in Armenian script

Evelyn Shamlian was the eldest daughter of Heranoush and Hagop Shamlian. She was born in Marash, Turkey, on September 16, 1910, and died in San Francisco on January 29, 1983.

My mother, Evelyn, was ten years old when the Battle of Marash occurred. Before that cataclysmic event, she remembered Marash as a wonderful place to explore with her brother, Toros. They saw the ruins, from the days of the Crusaders, of Frankish fortifications, and of castles near Marash. She never missed an opportunity to venture out and about with her brother. One morning early, they told their mother that they were going to the vineyards that their family owned. They didn't return in the afternoon or early evening either. The adults ended up getting together a search party to find and bring them back home. They were successful.

The one bad memory she had before the deportations of 1915 was of the Turkish boy who yanked her braids as she was walking to school and called her a giavoor or infidel. She retaliated by calling him, "You son of a pig."

The Shamlians were not immune to the upheaval surrounding them as one Armenian family after another was notified of deportation. Evelyn's family prepared for deportation on three different days. But after the third time, Evelyn's father was called to Turkish army headquarters and told he and his family would not be deported as the army needed the excellent leather produced by his tannery—the only Christian-owned tannery in Marash.

Before all of the life-changing events of 1915, Evelyn remembered her mother as a wonderful teacher. Whenever she was preparing meals, Heranoush would lovingly call her to her side and demonstrated the steps for a particular dish. Heranoush would encourage Evelyn to do the same. In this manner, Evelyn was taught to cook.

When the Battle of Marash began all of the Armenians in the Sheikh Mahallesi district congregated together to protect themselves and their neighborhood. For about ten days, they carried on but afterwards they realized they would have to get to safe quarters where French soldiers would protect them, and they would have access to food. Their goal was to get to the Latin Monastery.

Luckily for them a young Armenian American Legionnaire arrived in time to lead them to safety. Evelyn held onto Edward, her five-year-old brother, and with a small group of others they followed the young soldier. Quickly, they went through homes and alleyways. No one in their group panicked because the young soldier was so calm and self-assured.

When they arrived at their destination, other people from the neighborhood were there also. One night, at the monastery, Toros and Evelyn decided to sit on the ledge of one of the open windows to see what was happening to their beloved city. Armenian sections were ablaze and all night they heard screeching like the sounds of birds in distress. In the morning, they learned the sounds were of Armenians burned alive in their churches.

The after story to this horrendous battle appeared in the recollections of Evelyn's sister, Rebecca, and brother, Toros. No need to repeat it here. When the family did reach Aleppo, Syria, in 1921, they went first to a displaced persons camp. Evelyn remembered how filthy it was. There were well over two hundred Armenian refugees already there and one outhouse (latrine).

At Christmas, missionaries gave all the Armenian children gently used Christmas cards. Evelyn looked at the card with the Christmas tree and glitter and held it to her heart. It made her so happy to know there was such beauty in the world.

When the family was finally reunited with their father, Hagop, they still lived in poverty. Hagop was working for nearly nothing because of a dishonest employer. This was not unusual as Armenians, already residing in Aleppo, were taking advantage of the newly arrived refugees from Marash and other areas of Cilicia. Poor or not, Hagop wanted his daughters to be educated. His favorite sister, Ferideh, was now residing in Fresno, California. She left Marash for America after the Adana Massacre of 1909. When she came to Fresno, California, she experienced discrimination because of her

Armenian ancestry. Since she had light brown hair and was almost six feet tall, she passed herself off as a German and even called herself Frida. Eventually, she married a businessman who owned a packing house. Jim Vagim had lost both of his parents in the Hamidian Massacres of 1894-1896.

Ferideh and her brother, Hagop, corresponded back and forth and he asked for her help in paying for the education of his daughters. Ferideh got together with a group of women in Fresno who were originally from Marash. They collected money to send to Syria.

Unfortunately, most of this "scholarship" money was confiscated by the wealthier Armenians in the community. So both Evelyn and her sister Rebecca ended up doing janitorial work to pay for their tuition.

The sisters liked their classmates but the two of them were their own best friends. Evelyn was self-effacing to the point where she was almost paralyzed when it came to standing up for herself. Rebecca had no problems in that regard and would verbally go after those who were harassing her sister.

They loved going to school so much that the two to three miles to and from the American Girls' High School was not a problem. Their mother was never given the opportunity to attend school and she was so happy for her daughters and wanted them to look nice. She was also an excellent seamstress and, with what little money she was able to squirrel away, she bought material and made their clothes.

Every morning, the principal of the school Ms. Lucy Forman conducted prayer meetings, which meant a great deal to both sisters. Even so, they were very conscious of the gap between the wealthier girls and themselves.

One early evening as they were on their way to attend a function at the school, they were deluged by a severe rainstorm. By the time they reached their destination, their white knee-length stockings were covered in mud splatter. They sure didn't want to look shabby so they used their handkerchiefs and furiously wiped away as much of the mud as they could.

They loved school because it gave them purpose and so much satisfaction. Evelyn loved to laugh and had a wonderful sense of humor besides. An example was the time her class was presenting a concert in the school auditorium and there was a glitch in the proceedings on stage. The curtains were drawn and there was much commotion back stage. Finally, Evelyn popped her head out from between the curtains and called out in a loud voice, "That's all, folks." There was much laughter from the audience.

At this time, the mid to late 1920s, urgent messages were coming to the high school from outlying Armenian villages. "Teachers needed!" After Evelyn graduated, she accepted a position as a kindergarten through eighth-grade teacher in Birejik, Syria. Armenians were desperate that their children not forget their language and culture. Evelyn was prepared because of her excellent education at the high school.

When she arrived, she was a wisp of a girl. Eighteen years old and so thin a strong wind would blow her over. The women who welcomed her were aghast at her physique and were determined to "fatten her up." They need not have worried as Evelyn was now earning money with which to buy produce and was an excellent cook besides. Some of her wages were sent to her mother in Aleppo to pay for the education of her brother, Toros.

She loved her students and being independent. But not for long as her father, Hagop, was now in Iraq without his wife trying out another tanning opportunity. He needed a cook and housekeeper. He told Evelyn to come to Mosul. Before she left for Iraq, she returned home to gather up her belongings and it was then that her mother with much fanfare presented her with a gold ring with a tiny ruby. She told her daughter that she was now a "golden bracelet," so skilled she would never now or in the future have to sell family treasures so her family could get by.

Years later in 1962, my mother, Evelyn, gave me that same ring. I had just earned my teaching credential. Evelyn told me that I was now a "golden bracelet."

When Evelyn arrived to Mosul to take care of her father, there was also a need for teachers in that city. She applied and was hired as a teacher at the Armenian Apostolic church school in Mosul. She loved her job and her students but one comment she made really stood out. She said there wasn't one pretty girl in the entire school. Then she added, "The Turks sure took our prettier girls for themselves." The thought made her very angry. The following is a microcosm of the macrocosm of what happened to our girls and young matrons during the genocide of 1915. Evelyn recalled a trip that she took with her sister, Rebecca, to the town of Kirikhan in Syria. One Sunday, while worshipping in the exquisite Apostolic Church, they saw an incredibly beautiful woman with her head covered, worshipping along with the congregation. She was the wife of a wealthy Muslim Arab who let her practice her faith. It turned out she was an Armenian. Years later, in 2009, while traveling with a group of Armenians, I stepped into an enormous pile of rubble that was the same church or what was left of it—destroyed by the Turks.

The opportunities for meeting educated Armenian men were practically zero for Evelyn and Rebecca in Mosul. Their mother, Heranoush, felt she had to do something. Since her nephew, Dicran (a doctor), was married and living in Beirut, Lebanon, she wrote him a letter (with Evelyn taking dictation) asking a favor of him. She asked him to accept the girls as guests for a month and take them around Beirut and introduce them to eligible men. He accepted. Evelyn and Rebecca were so excited at the possibilities and even thought of training to become nurses in Beirut. Sometime earlier, Evelyn had apprenticed herself to a dressmaker and became very adept at creating patterns and making dresses. Looking at magazines that came from France, she saw the latest styles and was determined that the two of them would dress in high fashion while in Beirut. She sewed non-stop and even had Rebecca buy them a couple of parasols as she said that's what the stylish girls carried while walking along the boulevards. Since the Muslims of Mosul were very conservative, it was absolutely not appropriate for the two sisters to wear the stylish clothing that Evelyn sewed. But they could wear them in the more cosmopolitan Beirut.

They arrived in Beirut and were greeted warmly by their cousin, Dicran, who commented about how beautiful they were. His wife, Armine, on the other hand, announced that Beirut at that time of the year was not livable so the entire household (including servants) and all would be going to their summer home, which wasn't in Beirut. The girls were shocked to say the least. While there, the couple made a point of telling them that the Armenian girls who trained to be nurses in Beirut were nothing but tramps. So, for the entire month, they watched as their cousin and his wife exchanged affectionate comments and whispers. The girls did change into their beautiful dresses and walked around the grounds twirling their parasols. But there were no young men to appreciate their beauty or their talent. So they returned to Mosul and to their very disappointed mother.

However, Evelyn and Rebecca were not naive as their cousin and his wife probably thought they were. The following will do much to illuminate how well they were brought up and their strong moral fiber.

There was a brothel in Mosul and all of the prostitutes were Armenian girls. One of the most beautiful of these girls was Elise. As a youngster, she had been pushed into the life by an uncle. In Mosul, she was married to an Arab Christian who ran a pharmacy and was her pimp as well, encouraging men to go to the house where Elise plied her trade.

One day, unannounced, Elise paid a visit to the home of the Shamlians and, as shocked as the girls were by this uninvited visitor, they still offered her tea and pastries. Elise did a yeoman's job of encouraging the girls to visit the brothel, as she wanted to return their hospitality. Both Evelyn and Rebecca declined the invitation as they knew their reputations would be at risk if they were even seen entering the house.

When Evelyn, a few years later, was married to Sarkis Sarkisian, he told her everything about himself—no secrets. He said he had visited the brothel while a bachelor and that business was booming. The prostitutes catered to the fantasies and whims of the many men who frequented the brothel.

Years later in San Francisco, in the early 1960s when I was a student in College, the doorbell rang and I answered it. The middle-aged woman, deeply tanned with gray hair and stocky build, introduced herself as Elise and said she knew my mother and sister, Rebecca, in Mosul, Iraq. I told my mother she had a visitor and when the woman told my mother who she was my mother was shocked at the apparition from the past. Quickly my mother phoned her siblings and told them to come to dinner that night.

Elise arrived with her son who was in his twenties and a woman about the same age as Elise, not very attractive, who walked with a decided limp. It turned out that the other woman was a doctor and had performed numerous abortions on the prostitutes who worked in the brothel. I overheard my mother whispering to her sister, Rebecca, "What happened to Elise? She had the most beautiful creamy white skin and a beautiful figure."

My aunt Rebecca's husband, Arthur Yeranian, sat across from the doctor at the dining room table and grilled her about her degrees and where she worked as a medical professional. I could see the doctor was very uncomfortable. The lesson learned for me was that your reputation follows you throughout your life, wherever you are in the world. And that's what Evelyn and Rebecca knew in the very fiber of their beings even so many years ago when Elise attempted to lure the very smart sisters into a life of shame, unsuccessfully.

Evelyn Shamlian: What Happened to Her Afterwards

Eventually, Evelyn met a very attractive and charismatic man who happened to be a truck driver. Sarkis Sarkisian, aka "Deli Sarkis," was born in Keramet village near Iznik Lake, in the Southern Marmara Region of the Ottoman Empire in 1905. He experienced much loss and terror in his life. He survived the massive deportations in 1915 when Armenians were driven into the deserts of Syria and Mesopotamia. He lost everyone except for an older brother. Then in 1922, he had the misfortune to be in Smyrna just as Ataturk's army entered the city. Miraculously, he survived that inferno, too.

Sarkis was someone with very little formal education but was very articulate having learned the languages of people wherever he lived. Sarkis and Evelyn were married in the Armenian Apostolic Church in Mosul's old city in 1938.

Sarkis was politically astute because as he traveled the length and breadth of Iraq as a truck driver he ingratiated himself into Assyrian, Kurdish, and Arabic communities. He spoke their languages. Also, when he traveled for any length of time on his truck routes, he would be sure to bring home chickens, eggs, and other food stuffs that Evelyn would use to prepare meals—not only for the two of them but frequently for her family as well. My father noted that my mother had a very generous heart. Sarkis loved the country of Iraq and its people, my mother not so much. So it was a disappointment for him when he was told by a powerful Kurd in Mosul that he couldn't purchase land for an apple orchard, because he wasn't a Muslim. And this same Kurd even had Armenian ancestry going back generations.

Shortly after the meeting with the Kurd leader, Sarkis witnessed protests in Mosul's town center. Arabs with their swords raised aloft were screaming out for English (Christian) blood. This followed the death of Iraqi King Ghazi on April 3, 1939, under mysterious circumstances. Ghazi loved fast cars and was a good driver but unbelievably, to the Arabs, plowed his car head first into a lamppost. The Arab populace felt his death was a British plot as Ghazi advocated for Arab nationalism and even wanted to invade Kuwait to return it to Iraqi sovereignty.

Sarkis was upset at what he saw that day. Upon returning home, he told Evelyn, who was pregnant with me at the time, "We're not going through another blood bath like our people went through in 1915." I'm sure that Puzant, Evelyn's stepbrother, living in San Francisco, and having left Beirut, Lebanon, a number of years before learned by letter of that day's events. He wasted no time in beginning the process of getting his entire family out of Iraq, where they were all currently living.

So it was that in early 1941, Sarkis, Evelyn, infant son, Arthur Minas, born on November 9, 1940, and I, aged two, born on May 19, 1939, began our momentous journey to America. We arrived in August of 1941, six months after our initial departure from Mosul. The journey took so long because of numerous delays. Sarkis spent almost all of the money he had because of all the rescheduling. He only had $50.00 in his pocket at the end of the journey. Luckily, there were relatives who met us in San Francisco, so we weren't completely destitute and Sarkis was able to work.

My parents had two more children, Janet Anahid, born on July 23, 1943, and Lucille Catherine, born on September 9, 1947.

Both were born in San Francisco at St. Mary's Hospital.

Evelyn spent years as a housewife but saw that more money was needed for household expenses. She was a hardworking woman and, as luck would have it, got a job at the New Method Laundry on Seventeenth Street, one block from our home. She operated power sewing machines and repaired sheets from hotels around San Francisco. She was known to have pulled sheets out of mangles, turning almost upside down doing it. She loved her job and worked at the laundry for seventeen years and was heartbroken when it closed.

Evelyn attended Calvary Armenian Congregational Church when it was located at 1339 38th Avenue in San Francisco. My father taught her to drive so she wouldn't have to take public transportation. I sat in the back seat and remember his "lessons" on driving. Evelyn would sit in the driver's seat in her splendid green Chevrolet Impala and he sat next to her. Lesson one was how to drive out of the garage. So far, so good. Then he would begin barking out in Turkish, "Git, git, git" ("Go, go, go.") as she reversed the car. Lesson two was drive forward into the garage this time he shouted in Turkish, "Gel, gel, gel" ("Come, come, come"). His lessons continued in this manner until my mother felt she was ready for her driving test at the DMV. Not surprisingly, when she sat in the driver's seat next to the instructor, her leg shook so badly she had no control over her foot. Evelyn didn't pass. She took it one more time and got her license. Afterwards, she proudly drove over to Calvary Church every Sunday. And every Sunday she would sing in the choir under the spirited and exuberant leadership of Peter Amirkhanian. She loved being with the members of the choir and admired the choir leader, Peter, for his musicianship.

Evelyn was also the designated pilaf maker for all church dinners, which she did for years. I couldn't figure out how she knew the amount of water, rice, vermicelli, butter, and salt to use for such a humongous pot. But she did and her pilaf was delicious. She also used her talents as a seamstress, not only to create lovely outfits for herself, but also for her daughters. For the annual church bazaars that were fundraisers, she made aprons with her numerous fabric scraps. They quickly sold out. However, she was more ambitious and made beautiful pillows that she showed department store managers hoping to sell them on consignment. She felt encouraged at their response. Evelyn never forgot the poverty of her formative years in Aleppo, Syria. She regularly donated to the Armenian Missionary Association of America. My father and mother with other members of the AMAA spent a month in 1972 touring the mission centers of the organization. Istanbul and Yerevan were the highlights of their trip. However, Sarkis refused to go into the orphanage in Istanbul. I'm sure it would have reminded him of his own days in the orphanage in Mosul, Iraq.

In 1970, when I was in Istanbul on the tail end of my trip to Europe, I met my father's female cousins, Egsapet Baharyan (second cousin) and Armenouhie Atamian (first cousin). As I was attempting to converse in Armenian, Armenouhie spat out, "Stop! You are fracturing our Armenian language. And to think your mother, Evelyn wrote such exquisite letters in Armenian." I was ashamed of how my efforts to speak in Armenian met with such disdain but got over it. At the same time, I was curious about my mother's writing. Thankfully, I was able, after she died, to find a notebook with this notation on the first page in her hand. "This collection belongs to Miss Evelyn Shamlian, April 25, 1932." By 1932, Evelyn had already moved to Mosul, Iraq, to cook and clean for her father, Hagop. There is a possibility that she took a trip back to Aleppo, Syria and met up with some of her high school friends for the last time and had them write in this notebook.

Looking through the notebook, I found poems and literary quotations in Armenian written by Evelyn and her friends. When I studied her writing on page one, what stands out is Evelyn's total command of Armenian letters: the flourishes and freedom of her writing. She was twenty-two years old.

Throughout her life a love of heroes and heroines was an

important part of her nature. I remember, when I was an adolescent, mother singing a patriotic song about the heroes of Zeitoun. She would embellish the song with oom-pa-pas and end it on a very dramatic and abrupt conclusion. She also recalled fondly the young Armenian-American legionnaire who led her to safety during the battle of Marash in 1920.

Mother and her siblings were so proud of their father, Hagop. His heroic actions saved scores of Armenian boys and men from deportations and death during the years 1915-1918. How dispirited they all were when Stanley Kerr's book *The Lions of Marash* came out with just one sentence with his name and occupation and nothing about his heroism.

Thinking about her life, I understand now that you don't have to lead big armies and defeat your enemies in battle to be a hero. I remember as a child my mother taking all of us to the free clinic at St. Mary's hospital in San Francisco. We didn't have an appointment, so we would sit the whole day waiting to see a doctor. This is what families like ours, at poverty level, had to do since my father was not earning enough at his job to take care of a family of six. This happened frequently. She never complained while we waited, even though we children were bored out of our minds. As we got older, there were other important tasks ahead. My brother, Arthur, earned his AA Degree in Drafting from the City College of San Francisco.

Work was very important to both of my parents. My mother's brother-in-law, Arthur Yeranian, was an engineer at PG&E. So she made an appointment to see him. She wore her best coat and as she sat in his office she spoke very highly of my brother's abilities and talents. It took a while to convince Arthur Yeranian but he decided to take a chance and spoke to the personnel department. Arthur, the nephew, was soon hired.

I learned a great deal from my mother. She sacrificed her time and put her energies into making sure her children were healthy and productive. I don't ever remember her speaking of someone in a negative way. It was her day to day actions that made her a huge hero in my eyes.

CHAPTER 16
TESTIMONY OF REBECCA SHAMLIAN YERANIAN

Believe you can and you're halfway there
—Theodore Roosevelt

Arpine, Rebecca, and Arlene (left to right) with Baby Ellen (in front).
Mosul, Iraq 1941

Rebecca Yeranian was born on April 12, 1912, in the city of Marash, Turkey. She died on February 17, 2005, in San Francisco. Here is her recollection of the Marash War of 1920, as recorded by her niece, Ellen Sarkisian Chesnut, on December 22, 1987:

I remember one afternoon, a very brawny, tall Armenian volunteer (a gamavor) came into the courtyard of our house and started looking around. Suddenly, a shot rang out and the man fell over dead. He was killed by a Turkish soldier who had spotted him from another building. The Battle had begun. We quickly dragged him by his boots into the house. My half sister, Helen, who was nineteen years old at the time, became hysterical.

"Oh my god, if the Turks can kill a soldier just like that, what will happen to me? I'll be raped and forced into a harem!"

Nothing we could do would calm her down. She even refused to eat and wouldn't talk to anyone. In desperation, Helen was disguised and taken to the Girl's College in Marash. My mother didn't want the Turks to see her as she was a very beautiful girl. Our house was very vulnerable to attack being in an important and elevated position in the Sheikh-Mahallesi district; so we had to get to one of the safe military centers in the city. We waited for the longest time until we were finally notified of the evacuation. An Armenian volunteer came to take us to a safe refuge. My mother, Heranoush, told us to quickly grab whatever quilts we could. The volunteer thought it best that we not all leave together. My sister, Evelyn, was in the group led by the legionnaire. She was holding the hand of her brother, Edward. My mother was carrying Isgouhi on her back while I carried the quilts.

We couldn't keep up with the others and began to go over the same trail. My mother realized what was happening and, in her panic, she kept saying over and over again, "Ya, Hesus!" I saw how scared she was and I became frightened too and began repeating "Ya Hesus" with her.

A man saw us and called out, "What are you doing out here?" My mother replied, "We're lost. Please help us. We're going round in a circle."

"Quick, follow me!" he said. "I'll get you to safety."

We followed him in the dark. Snow covered the ground; the night sky was lit up by cannon fire. My heart was beating very fast as I held onto my mother's hand. Thank goodness someone had come to rescue us. We climbed higher and higher until we saw the Latin Monastery. Our refuge.

When we got inside, there were so many families huddled together but I did see my father and the rest of the family. What a happy moment. But there was ominous news. In early February, my father found out that the French soldiers were going to withdraw from the city. Turkish authorities had warned my father that there were fifty gold pounds on his head. He would be executed if he stayed. He decided to leave with the retreating French. My father kissed us all goodbye and left us in the care of my mother.

Three thousand Armenians, men, women and children followed the French into a blizzard, one of the worst in a century. My father was wearing an old pair of leather shoes. Shivering, he rubbed his arms and moved along with the rest of the group. Suddenly, a woman sunk down in the snow in front of him. He went over to her and saw she was very pregnant. When he asked her where her husband was, she replied that she didn't know. He called to a man riding on a horse and asked him if he would let the woman ride as she could no longer walk. The man agreed. Grandfather lifted her onto the horse and stayed with her until they reached the train station and boarded. A pitiful remnant of the original group reached this destination. Many had dropped in the snow and froze to death, their clothing removed by survivors.

Sometime later, the train was attacked by bandits and derailed. The hapless passengers then walked to Adana. Only about half of the people who had started out from Marash reached Adana. My father dragged himself to the hospital where it was obvious that his feet were so badly frostbitten that gangrene had set in. He would have to face amputation. My father would not accept the doctor's diagnosis and told him, "You better take that knife and cut my throat. Do you know how many people are depending on me?" One of the nurses began to treat his feet and was able to save them.

Back in Marash, at the monastery, I became very ill and wouldn't touch any food. The only thing I craved was raisins. My mother went from family to family asking if there were any raisins to spare. None! My half-brother, Hrant, seeing how upset I was, snuck out of the monastery to get raisins. He was on his way back to our house in the Sheikh-Mahallesi district when some Turks, who knew that he was Shamlian's son and an epileptic, got ahold of him and took him back up to the monastery; in the midst of the hostilities there were kind-hearted Turks who thought enough of my grandfather to look after Hrant. When they delivered him to my mother, they reprimanded her for letting him out. She told them that she had no idea he had gone.

Shortly after the French had withdrawn from Marash, the mon père of the monastery told the Armenians who were still there that we would be better off if we went to the American Girls' College. Our family went over to the college and they put us into the music room. I remember because there was a piano. Once a week, my sister, Evelyn, went to the Armenian in charge of the destitute families to ask for financial help. When Haidos Hodja asked her how many were in our group, she replied, "Twenty, sir." He would exclaim, "Twenty! Abov!" (Wow!)

I don't recall how long we stayed but after a while the fighting in the city stopped and we left the college and moved over to a very large house owned by the Bilesjekjian family. We were able to rent a room in that large house along with other destitute families. It was there that my sister Isgouhi died. There was an epidemic of measles and that's what killed my little sister. She was four years old. She spoke Turkish with us like a grownup and always inquired as to what was going on. You couldn't keep a secret from her. She was sorely missed by all of us.

With much difficulty, my father made it to Beirut where his eldest son and my half-brother, Puzant, was studying chemistry at the American University. A student told Puzant, who was very concerned about his family in Marash, the news about the French abandonment of the city, and there was an Armenian man wearing tattered clothing who was inquiring about him. Puzant saw that the man was his father, Hagop. They had a very emotional reunion.

Puzant and a fellow student were going to go to America and tried to convince Hagop to go with them but there was no way that Hagop would leave his family. He went to Aleppo, Syria where he found a job as a tanner and started to send us money. Unfortunately, much of it did not get through to us.

We stayed in the Bilesjekjian house until mother's money ran out. When it finally happened, she said, "If I'm going to die, I'd like to die under my own roof. C'mon children, we're going home."

One night, we all went back to our house in the Sheikh Mahallesi district of Marash. Hrant was seventeen years old. Toros was thirteen years. Evelyn was ten years old. I was eight and Edward was six years old. Someone was living downstairs but was not home. The front door was open. We tiptoed in and followed mother upstairs to the second floor. This was the floor that had not been finished by my grandfather. Crawling under the big quilt we brought with us, we fell asleep. During the night, as we were sleeping, mother cried, "Oooooh, oooooh, oooooh" in her sleep. The more she cried the closer we snuggled against her. Finally, I woke up and said, "Mom, wake up!" She sat up and said that she was having nightmares.

In the morning, the Turkish army officer who had moved into our house with his wife and in-laws confronted my mother and told her that in the middle of the night he had heard a moaning upstairs and slowly came up the stairs and saw all of us asleep under the large quilt.

He drew back his sword to kill us but he told us that something held onto his arm and literally prevented him from doing so. Somehow mother convinced him that all of us could live under the same roof. He let us use the house and sleep in the stable. But, he was not a very good person. He had a pretty wife and yet he brought prostitutes home. My mother reprimanded him about that.

Oftentimes, I remember how his wife and mother would cower behind our mother when he threatened to hit them. He grew to respect our mother and began calling her Maryam (Arabic form of Mary), a name of respect.

I remember also how Hrant would help carry the wheat for our mother when she went to the market. Toros, my other brother, worked as a weaver to earn a little money for the family. But he very quickly tired of that and stopped, as he wanted to go to school.

When the Armenian Orthodox Church established a school for the children who remained in Marash, Toros and

Evelyn got to go. They wouldn't let me but I carried on so much about not wanting to be illiterate that I finally got to go, too.

We lived like this for six months until my father was able to hire a carriage and a covered wagon in Aleppo. The Arab drivers came to Marash for us. We climbed on board and were joined by mother's first cousin Mihranoosh der Muggerdichian, her two daughters and a son. Once in a while we would stop at way stations but the drivers did not like how the Turkish and Kurdish men were eyeing the girls so they told my mother that the teenaged girls would have to be hidden. So Helen and our two girl cousins were at certain points of the journey hidden under quilts and we would sit on them to make it look as if the quilts were covering the cushions.

Life in Syria was very difficult for our family. My father was not flush with money as he had been in Marash. Yet, even under those trying circumstances, he was determined to send his daughters to school. So my sister, Evelyn, and I were sent to the American missionary school. Tuition was paid for by Marashtzi women in America.

Evelyn and I worked for our tuition by scrubbing floors, windows and emptied garbage cans. Oftentimes, we went to school hungry and did not even bring a lunch with us as there was hardly any food in the house. When the other girls ate lunch, we pretended that we had already eaten and continued playing in the schoolyard. One time, Evelyn passed out from hunger in the classroom and, another time, I had a lesson totally prepared but, when called upon by the teacher, I couldn't remember a thing. I attribute that to hunger. My father good to his word continued to get help from his sister, Ferideh Vagim, in Fresno, for our tuition so we could attend the American Girls High School in Aleppo, Syria. Unfortunately, the money sent for our tuition was taken by the wealthier students in the school.

We walked two to three miles to school every day. I remember fondly the principal of our school, Ms. Lucy Forman, and the morning prayer meetings.

On our summer vacations, my sister, Evelyn, and I would do Aintab work on handkerchiefs. Turvant Hanum would inspect the handkerchiefs. She would give us the material and we would do the edging. When finished we would give her the handkerchiefs. We were paid for each piece. Then our work was sent to the United States. In this way, we helped our family. Evelyn would take what money she earned, go to the market, and buy fruit for the family.

Evelyn and I spent so many wonderful years learning. In 1929, I had the good fortune to participate in my graduating class's production of Shakespeare's "The Merchant of Venice." I played the part of Antonio. My school years were a glorious part of my life. I honor the memory of my father for sending us to school.

CHAPTER 17
RECOLLECTIONS OF
EDWARD SHAMLIAN

Tell me and I forget, teach me and I may remember,
involve me and I learn.
—Benjamin Franklin

Edward Shamlian, Mosul, Iraq, 1937

E dward Shamlian was the youngest son of Hagop and
Heranoush Shamlian. Edward was born in Marash, Turkey on
September 1, 1915. He died on April 5, 1991, in San
Francisco.

The following recollections are from phone conversations with his
niece, Ellen Sarkisian Chesnut, on July 24, 1990, March 20, 1991, and
March 24, 1991:

In February 1920, with my father gone as he had followed the retreating French troops out of Marash, my mother, Heranoush, became the head of the family. We were staying along with other families in the Bilesjekjian residence but our money was running out. My mother went to the police station and received permission to return to our home (now taken over by a Turk). We moved back and went first to the second floor. Because there was no place to relieve ourselves, mother told us boys to urinate from the balcony.

The Turk had a wife and in-laws living with him and yet he would bring prostitutes home. My mother was fed up as she had young children, so she reported him to the police. When they came for him, he escaped by running over rooftops.

While all of this was going on in Marash, my father, Hagop, survived amputation of his feet at the hospital in Adana. A female nurse took care of him there, saving his feet, though toes that had gangrene were amputated. After the hospitalization, he managed to get to the American University of Beirut (in Lebanon) where his eldest son, Puzant, was studying chemistry. One of Puzant's professors, Mr. Charles Perrine, saw the bedraggled Hagop and offered him a job as janitor. That was not in the realm of possibilities for him. He declined. Then Mr. Charles Perrine offered to pay for passage to America for both Hagop and Puzant. He wouldn't do that either because, as he said everybody in Marash would talk about how he abandoned his family. Hagop decided that Puzant must go to America, work and get the rest of the family out of Turkey and to the United States.

With Puzant gone, Hagop left Beirut and went to Zahlé, close to Baalbek, and opened a tannery there. Aram Mississian, whom he saved from deportation in the years 1915-1916, worked for him. Then Hagop left Zahlé and went to Halep (Aleppo). In later years, Hagop knew that had been a poor decision, as he would have made a good living in Lebanon.

In the meantime, Puzant had a job in America and started to send money to our father. With that money, my father got us out of Marash. At first, in Aleppo, we lived in a displaced persons camp with over two hundred people living in deplorable conditions.

I was a six-year-old kid, standing in a very long line to use the outhouse. It was winter and freezing cold, so cold that I was barely able to take my penis out of my pants to urinate. My hands were blocks of ice.

Somehow, with the little money coming in, my parents managed to send us all to school. Every day after school, I walked three miles to where my father worked as a tanner to help with chores and mostly take water from the well.

Dishonest Armenians were taking advantage of the newly arrived from Turkey. My father worked for Hovannes, from morning until 8:00 at night. Tanning is backbreaking work, so my father quit. Then he met an Armenian who sold beef to the French army and went into partnership with him, contracting to get the hides of the animals. But first he needed vets or holes in which to cure the leather. An Armenian, originally from Dikranagerd (now known as Diyarbekir) had a tannery and rented out the vets to Hagop. However, the man was a cheat. When the hides that Hagop cured were put on the market, they brought in a pitiful amount of money. The truth was the owner was selling Hagop's hides as his own and substituting his inferior hides as Hagop's.

The good news was that, with the money my brother was sending us from America, we were able to pay rent on a house and Dr. Philip Ovannian took care of our medical needs at no charge. My cousin, Arsen Topalian, roomed with us. He gave what he could to help us financially but, we were so poor, his contributions hardly made a dent and left Arsen with little or no spending money for himself.

His mother, Csanna, who was my father Hagop's eldest sister was widowed with four children. During the Battle of Marash and afterward, she worked as a maid for the American missionary. She stayed on in Marash until 1925. Most of the Armenians had, by then, immigrated out of there.

Arsen was a remarkable young man and had, what I considered, to be a photographic memory. He would read something and immediately recall it. I remember, at night, when all of us were lying on the floor under the quilts, Arsen would tell us stories. One of them was Victor Hugo's Les Misérables. The best part about it was that Arsen would tell the story with all the details intact. I also remember, at 10:00

p.m. sharp, he would stop even though we implored him to continue. We were all attending school and he didn't want to keep us up too late.

The one incident that triggered Arsen's disenchantment with Aleppo was on a carnival night, when all the Arab Christians were in costume, Arsen grabbed a hat from one of the revelers and ran with it. A group of them ran after him in hot pursuit. He was certain, if they had caught up with him, they would have killed him.

It was soon after that episode he told my mother, Heranoush, that he would be immigrating to Sao Paolo, Brazil. Many Armenians were, at this time, leaving Aleppo for Brazil. He left with a young man who was an in-law of the Chakmakjian family. Shortly after their arrival in Brazil, this boy had an appendicitis attack and Arsen had no idea what was happening. He died in Arsen's arms. Arsen wrote to my mother and we all remember what he told her, "Auntie, I'm not the same Arsen that you knew. My legs don't have any strength in them. They're wobbly."

Well, my mother immediately asked around and was able to get some herbs from an herbologist. These herbs were sent to Arsen in the hopes that his condition would improve.

He had a business in Sao Paolo. He would sell clothes as a traveling merchant, going from village to village in Brazil. Then, he decided he wanted to try his hand at farming, so he gave up the clothing business. But I remember he wrote to us and said farming in Brazil was extremely difficult. One day, you would put sulfur on your crops and the next day there would come a torrential rain and ruin all of your hard work so that you would have to start all over again.

Arsen did bring his mother and sister, Rose, to Brazil. Rose married an Armenian man shortly after her arrival, but nine months later, he abandoned her. She never remarried. Years before, their brother, Ebeneezer, had immigrated to the United States and, while working in a sheet metal factory, stepped onto a rusty nail, got lockjaw, and died.

Arsen meant a great deal to all of us. He left such an indelible impression. I wonder what he would have accomplished in totally different circumstances.

Meanwhile, things started to shift for my father as he met

an Armenian financier, by the name of Gayiklian, in Aleppo. He offered my father and two other men the chance to make a living in Mosul, Iraq—one was a coppersmith and the other, Partramian, was a cigarette manufacturer.

Hagop left the family and journeyed to Mosul by himself. He was a bachelor for a while but couldn't fix his meals, so he told my sister, Evelyn, to come to Mosul to help him. She cooked his meals and helped him with household matters. She also got a position as a school teacher in an Armenian Apostolic Church school.

In 1932, the whole family came to Mosul. My father worked in partnership with another tanner, renting three vets, from an Arab tanner, and I continued helping him at the tannery, which was like the ones in Aleppo, way out of town.

I worked at the tannery from 1933 to 1941. Because of the chemicals in the tanning vets, I had no hair on my legs as the chemicals burned the hair off.

The coppersmith who had come to Mosul with my father eventually relocated to South America. Everybody pitched in financially to help the family, including my brother, Toros, who worked as an engineer in the oil fields. He gave 15 dinars a month to my father.

The situation in Iraq was getting to be precarious for Christians because of the political climate and the hostility the Arabs felt toward the English. It was time to leave.

So, in 1941, my sister, Rebecca, and I bought passage on the ship called the M.S. Bloemfontein. It seemed like wherever we docked, Rebecca had proposals of marriage. In Mosul, she was engaged to a widower who had five children. But she told him that, if the opportunity came to go to America, she would have to get out of the engagement.

When we docked in India, she received a proposal of marriage from an Armenian merchant; then, in Singapore, another proposal—this time from the owner of the famous Raffles hotel and a member of the Sarkies family.

My brother-in-law, Sarkis Sarkisian, his wife, Evelyn (who was my eldest sister), and their two children, Shakeh and Minas, were on the M.S. Boschfontein. Also on the same ship as Evelyn and Sarkis, were my brother, Toros, and his wife, Arpine.

*　　　　　*　　　　　*

Edward Shamlian: What Happened Afterwards

The first job Edward had in San Francisco was at the Cadillac Company, in their auto body division. He worked there for a number of years, all the while thinking about getting married. Roxie Shirinian, from Sanger, California and Edward met through mutual friends in San Francisco. This was after he wrote her a letter stating that he wanted to meet her, as it was known that she was from a good family and of Armenian heritage. He traveled back and forth to Sanger from San Francisco as he courted her. Eventually, they were engaged. However, Roxie found out after the engagement that he had lied about his age. He was, in reality, thirteen years older than her. She called off the engagement and gave back the engagement ring. Edward went back to Sanger many times and, after numerous apologies, she accepted his ring. Roxie's family had convinced her that he would be a good husband and provider. When Roxie was dating Edward, she received a package in the mail. Excitedly, she opened it and discovered an 8x10-framed picture of Edward. He wanted Roxie to keep him utmost in her mind as she had other eligible men interested in her. Roxie kept that picture of Edward on her dresser in her bedroom until the day she died.

Edward and Roxie married in San Francisco at Trinity Methodist Church at 16th and Market Streets on October 9, 1948. Richard Kazarian, the husband of Edward's youngest sister Arlene (aka Isgouhi) was the best man. The wedding was a gala and happy affair with many friends and relatives in attendance.

While their new home was being built on Diamond Street in San Francisco, Edward and Roxie lived in an apartment. When they moved into their new home, they had three children: Dennis was born on January 13, 1951; Janet (Ishkanian) was born on April 2, 1953; and Debra (Abajian) was born on April 12, 1955.

As the children grew older, their father decided it was time to venture out on his own and become self-employed. Edward purchased an auto body shop with a partner in the downtown area of San Francisco. He encouraged his children to come up with a name for his business. It was decided that Central Auto Body Repair was the best choice. Edward worked hard even though his job was very taxing on him physically. He had great pride in his workmanship and instilled his work ethic in his children. Roxie was a stay-at-home mom and loved to cook and bake. It was important for both her and Edward that she do this as the children were growing up. However, finances were a challenge as she was given a small sum of money with which to purchase items needed for the family. Roxie wanted to do more for her children like give them piano, ballet, and dance lessons, and involvement in Little League Sports. She decided to apply for a job, which consisted of driving a double sun-roofed white limousine that advertised President Johnson's image, one of 135 new figures that would help open the redecorated Wax Museum at Fisherman's Wharf. Roxie drove around San Francisco's financial district with the sunroof open and a wax statue of Lyndon B. Johnson peering out of the sunroof. Many people commented with considerable fanfare that it was Ladybird Johnson who was driving the vehicle. An article was printed in the San Francisco Chronicle in 1964 with the title, "I'm Melting, Folks!"

Later on, Roxie worked at the Emporium in the bookkeeping department and, in this way, contributed to helping with household expenses. Edward and Roxie were active at Calvary Armenian Congregational Church in San Francisco. Church and family were of utmost importance to them along with their Armenian heritage.

Edward and Roxie only spoke Armenian when there was "secret" information they wanted to discuss between themselves. Mostly they conversed in English. Occasionally, Edward used a few choice Turkish words when he wanted to express his disdain for something.

All of the children concurred that the best days of their lives growing up were the camping trips the family took in the summers to national parks in the western United States. To make it even more special, Richard and Arlene Kazarian and their children frequently accompanied them.

CHAPTER 18

ARLENE SHAMLIAN KAZARIAN

Arlene was the youngest child of Hagop and Heranoush Shamlian. She was born in Aleppo, Syria, on September 16, 1925, and died in northern California on September 6, 2016.

She was born five years after the Battle of Marash. She recalled some childhood experiences in Mosul, Iraq, where the family relocated after living in Aleppo, Syria, during the 1920s. Arlene started her education in an Armenian school in Mosul and then was transferred to the local Arab Christian school. She remembered the principal who was an Arab and incredibly beautiful. Some of the Arab girl students had head lice so the principal would rub their scalps with gasoline.

Arlene came to America from Iraq on the M.S. Bloemfontein. Her trip to America took 63 days On January 1941, the ship docked in San Pedro, California where relatives were there to meet her. Sometime later in June of 1941, Edward and Rebecca also arrived in San Francisco.

Arlene attended Girls' High School in the Western Addition district of San Francisco. Her brother, Edward, introduced her to Richard Kazarian, whose parents, Khoomar and Gregory, were both born in Urumia, Persia. Both died years later in San Francisco. Arlene's husband, Richard, was born on October 27, 1921, and died on July 7, 2012.

Arlene and Richard were married in the 1940s. They had three children: Al, Susan, and Carol.

Words of Remembrance for Arlene Kazarian

Written in loving memory by Janet Shamlian Ishkanian, Arlene's niece and the daughter of Edward and Roxie Shaman on September 13, 2016:

> President Abraham Lincoln, in talking about his mother once said, "All that I am or ever hope to be, I owe to my angel Mother." I believe this quote is applicable for an aunt, as well.
>
> It is so difficult to summarize the life of someone you've known for so many years without trivializing that person's life. When I think about Auntie Arlene, a question always comes to mind, "What could I say that would acknowledge and share both our joy in the gift that her life was to us, and the sorrow that her passing brings?" In sharing the joy and sorrow together today, may we lessen the sadness and remember more clearly the joy.
>
> Aunt Arlene was an angel, a wonderful wife, mother, grandmother, sister-in-law, aunt, and friend. She was one of the most wonderful people that I will ever know. She was one of my favorite aunts.
>
> Aunt Arlene had a small frame, but what she lacked in size she made up for in personality. She had such a large presence. She spoke with her hands and her heart. She always had an opinion, and she wasn't shy about sharing it. Her strength of character helped her in raising her three children, Alvin, Carol and Susan, to be individuals with very strong senses of self.
>
> She had a distinct personal style and was totally in charge, and we all knew it—her elaborate table settings for gatherings, her skill at the art of presentation during dinners at her home, her amazing organization, her personal dress and demeanor, her acute knowledge and wisdom. She had a way about her that was so very special.
>
> Auntie Arlene was a devout Christian and was a prayer. I'm sure she prayed for everyone in this room at some time in her life, her family and her friends. It was her strong faith that carried her through challenging times in her life and, on the morning she passed, it was her faith and trust that guided

Auntie Arlene so gracefully and peacefully from our hands to God's.

As a child I remember visiting my Aunt Arlene frequently whether it be attending birthday parties, holiday gatherings, life events, and the many marathon visits, which lasted hours. We were always happy to see our cousins. My mother and her sister-in-law were very close, which meant we were able to spend a lot of time with my cousins, Aunt and Uncle, and for that I am grateful. I knew as soon as we approached their home in San Francisco on 9 Homewood Court, the fun would begin, once you got passed the German shepherd, Fritz, who was guarding the front door and barking wildly upon hearing our footsteps. My Uncle Dick would give Fritz a command, and that would settle him right down, right next to my mother, as though he were guarding her, as well.

Auntie Arlene greeted us with a big smile and a robust hug. Delicious treats were always served, as Aunt Arlene was a wonderful cook. She would sometimes make food magically appear on the table when you least expected it. As kids, we were guaranteed many hours of playtime, as the adults discussed matters of importance. Our evenings always included sitting around the kitchen table and listening for the last kernel of popcorn to be popped, whereby my Aunt would give each of us a handful in a bowl, followed by a special treat of chewing gum that was located in a See's Candy box tucked away in one of the kitchen drawers.

Since Aunt Arlene and my mother were both such wonderful cooks, there was a rivalry that took place consistently between the two of them when it had to do with Yalanchi, yes, Yalanchi. For those of you who do not know what Yalanchi is, it is Armenian stuffed grape leaves. I was witness to their competitive spirit on many occasions. Aunt Arlene always insisted that the best rice to use was Uncle Ben's and my mother fiercely argued that it was MJB rice. This playful competition went on for years. To this day, when I shop and stand in the aisle looking at the shelves of rice, I too ponder, which rice is the best. Inevitably, I choose Uncle Ben's in the spirit of Auntie Arlene.

Another special memory that I have of my Aunt Arlene and Uncle Dick, were during the days when we camped at national parks side-by-side. These were days of laughter, hikes, campfires with the park rangers, and playing cards next to a Coleman lantern into the wee hours of the night. I'll never forget the special time when I was asked to go with my cousins to Yosemite National Park—without my parents or siblings. I was filled with excitement at the invitation. However, I knew from experience, that both my mother and Aunt Arlene had very high standards, especially when it came to entering the "sacred" tent. I knew the routine; one that I had secretly hoped my Aunt Arlene would forget... the ritual of the cold-water scrub! Each of us would sit on the picnic table, and she would start at one end and scrub our faces, hands and feet before we were allowed to enter the tent and climb into our sleeping bags. There were squeals of laughter and moans from the bitter cold of the water. Nothing will ever diminish those wonderful and loving memories that I have of our camping days.

My aunt had a way of making people feel special. She listened intently to everything that you said to her and weighed in with her opinion. She really cared. She established friendships with those who attended her church, her neighbors, and those she walked and exercised with at the Hillsdale Mall. Aunt Arlene was a constant support for all who knew her, especially her wonderful grandchildren.

I am grateful for being part of my Aunt Arlene's life. She was more than an aunt to me; she was a friend. I will miss our long talks on the phone, and all of the time we spent together during my annual summer visits. Auntie Arlene holds a special place in the hearts of her nieces, nephews, family and friends. Her memory will live on in my heart forever. I will miss her more than words can say.

I would like to leave you all with this poem and most especially words for Alvin, Carol, and Susan:

"Your Mother Is Always With You"

Your mother is always with you...
She's the whisper of the leaves as you walk down the street.

She's the smell of bleach in your freshly laundered socks.
She's the cool hand on your brow when you're not well.

Your mother lives inside your laughter.
She's crystallized in every tear drop...

She's the place you came from, your first home.
She's the map you fol ow with every step that you take.

She's your first love and your first heart break...
and nothing on earth can separate you.

Not time, Not space...
Not even death...
will ever separate you from your mother...

You carry her inside of you...

CHAPTER 19

THERE ARE INVISIBLE GUESTS

O n January 18, 1986, I visited my Uncle Toros, my mother Evelyn's older brother, at his home in San Mateo, California. At that time, he was married to his second wife, Rosine; his first wife, Arpine, had died some years before.

I spent the morning interviewing my uncle about his experiences during the Battle of Marash in 1920. Rosine invited me to stay for lunch. She had also been born in Marash in 1914. Her family had experienced terrible episodes during the Genocide of 1915 and had immigrated to Egypt after the Great Crime.

Rosine said whenever her relatives got together they would cry about the family and friends they had lost. This happened for years. The grieving never ended.

That's why I have chosen to end the book with a poem written in 1915 by the great Armenian poet, Yeghishe Charentz (1897-1937). He was born Yeghishe (Elisha) Soghomonian, and grew up in Kars which is 520.6 miles from Marash. Like all Armenians throughout the length and breadth of the Ottoman Empire, the Armenians of Kars and Marash experienced mass violence and political chaos; however, there is no violence depicted in the poem "There Are Invisible Guests" written in 1915—just a feeling of overwhelming loss.

Yeghishe Charentz
(There Are Invisible Guests)

Translated by David Kherdian and Garig Basmadjian

There are invisible guests. They enter
without speaking, and fall into the lap
of silence. They appear, they live,
and then they pass by. We neither open
a door for them, nor do we close one.

They are without name or shadow.
Nor do they make a sound.
They come, they live, and then silently disappear.
And why did they come, and why did they go?
What are we to make of that amorphous world?

Only this: that when an endless and deep sadness
spreads its wings everywhere,
we feel suddenly with an immense yearning
that someone has passed never to return.

1915

Կան Անտես Հյուրեր

Կան անտես հյուրեր։ Գալիս են նրանք
Անխոս ու անձայն, լռութեան ծոցում։
Գալիս են, ապրում ու անցնում նրանք՝
Ոչ դուռ են բացում եւ ոչ դուռ գոցում։

Ո՛չ անուն ունեն, ո՛չ ստվեր, ո՛չ ձայն։
Գալիս են, ապրում եւ անցնում են լուռ։
Եվ ինչո՞ւ եկան, եւ ինչո՞ւ անցան –
Մենք չենք իմանում աշխարհում անդուռ։

Միայն մի անձայր ու խոր տխրություն
Երբ փռում է իր թեն ամենուրեք –
Զգում ենք հանկարծ կարոտով անհուն,
Որ մեկը անդարձ անցել է երեկ...

1915

PHOTOS

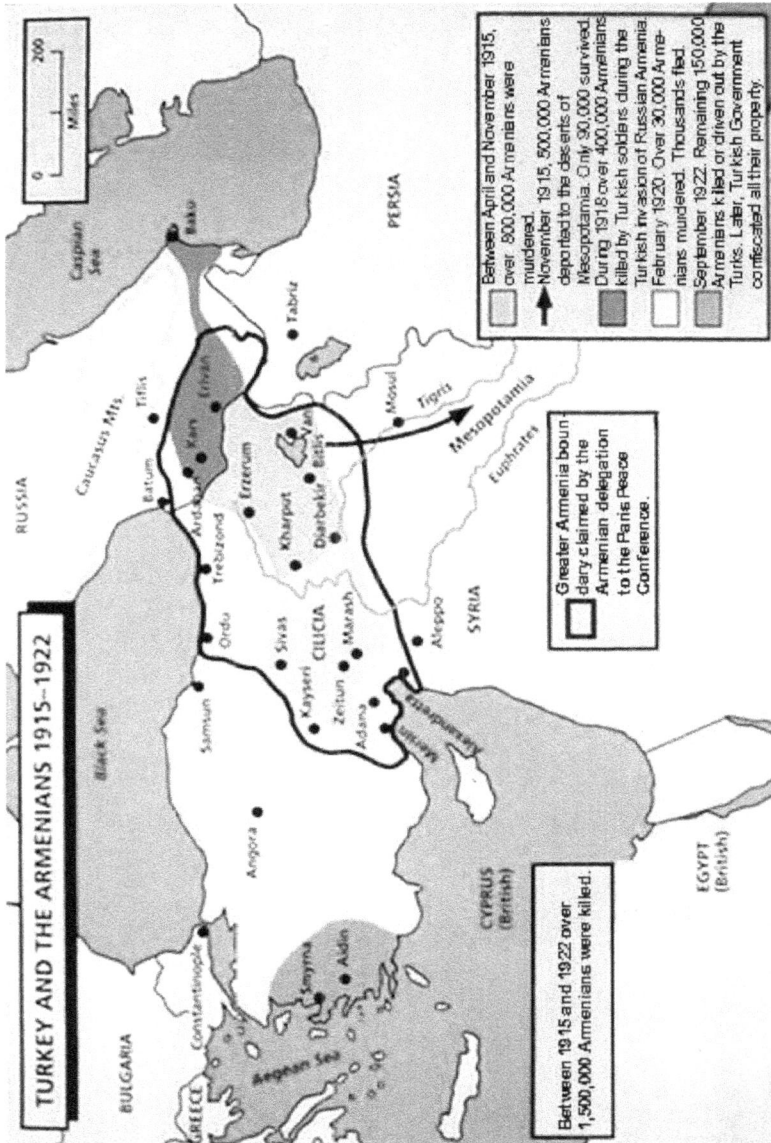

Map: Turkey and the Armenians 1915-1922.

Turkey Photos

An artist's rendering of Marash in 1700.

Marash in 2016.

Ellen in Kahramanmaras (Marash) in 2009.

Multi media art: Battle of Marash done by Ellen in 1989.

Armenian Legionnaires, Marash, 1920.

Stanley Kerr in Marash (wearing the light colored uniform).

Yeranian store in Marash: February 14, 1910. On bag translated: bibles, Avedis Yeranian on left, Sarkis (his eldest son) sitting in store, customer on right.

German Hospital, Marash, 1910.

Toros Shamlian, the father of Hagop Shamlian.

Abraham Berberian, teacher, expert in calligraphy, minister and father of Dicran Berberian.

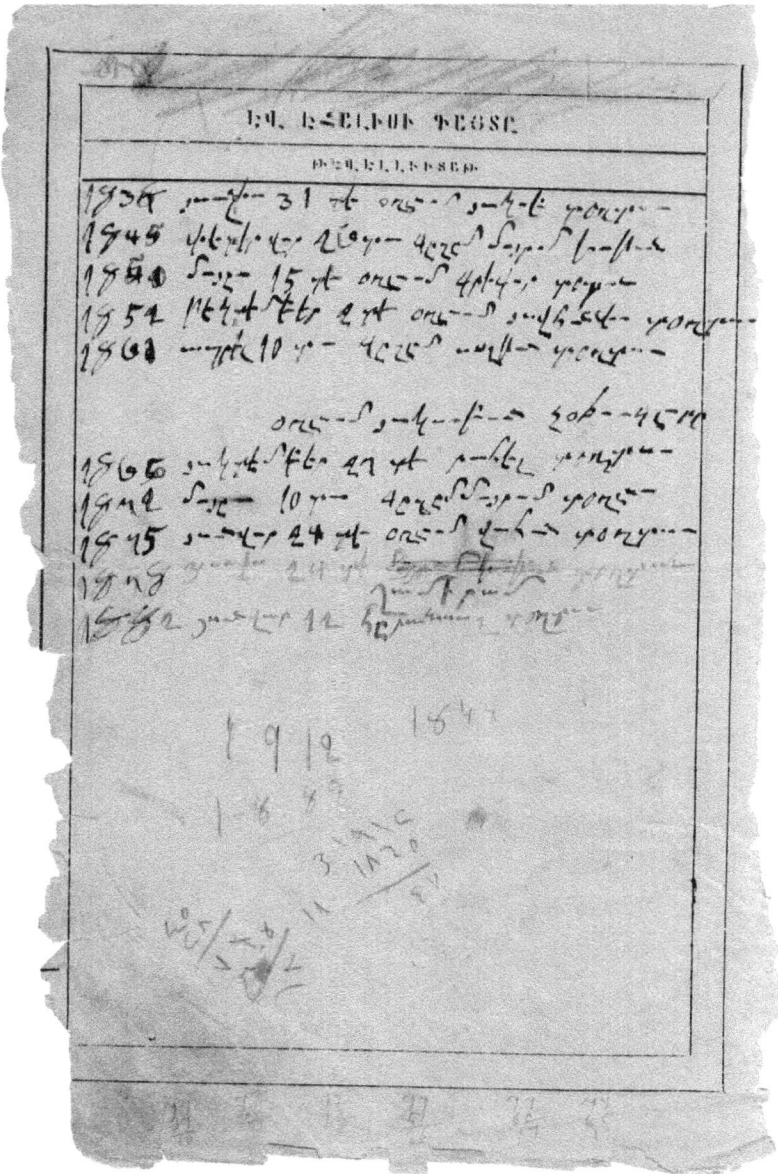

Nalbandian births in family bible written in Armenian: Hagop Nalbandian was the father of these siblings: 1866 — Dec 27 Rahel was born. 1872 — May 10 Miriam was born. 1875 Jan 24 Vahan was born. 1878 — July 24 Shamiram was born. 1882 — Jan 12 Heranoush was born.

Dicran's mother Shamiram Berberian, (back row left),
her sister Heranoush (front row right), and his other aunts.

Three Families, Marash, Turkey, 1920 or 1921. Front row center: Edward Shamlian, Second row: left to right: Evelyn Shamlian, Osanna Topalian, Heranoush Shamlian, Rebecca Shamlian. 3rd row, left to right: Haroutune Berberian, Hrant Shamlian, Arsen Topalian, Rose Topalian, Helen Shamlian, Toros Shamlian, Dicran Berberian.

Marash, Turkey 1911. Hagop Shamlian's family: front row: left to right, Hrant, baby Evelyn sitting on her grandmother Izgouhi's lap, Toros next to her. Second row: left to right: Hagop's sister, Osanna Shamlian Topalian, his sister, Ferdie Shamlian Vagim, Hagop, his second wife, Heranoush, Puzant next to her.

Syria Photos

Aleppo, Syria, 1921. Evelyn (top row left)
and Rebecca (bottom row second from right) in school.

Aleppo, Syria. Evelyn on far right with classmates on outing (late 1920s).

Aleppo, Syria, 1929. Students in the American Girls' High School performing Shakespeare's "The Merchant of Venice." Rebecca (fifth from left) as Antonio.

Evelyn in American Girls' High School, Aleppo, Syria 1920s: Second row, second from right.

Mosul, Iraq, 1929. Armenian Apostolic Church school.
Evelyn—teacher (second row, second from left).

Mosul, Iraq, 1938. Left to right: Toros, Rebecca, Arpine, Arlene, Evelyn, Sarkis.

Mosul, Iraq Photos

Mosul, Iraq, 1937: From left: Rebecca, Heranoush, Arlene, unknown children. Evelyn holding hands with friend.

Toros and Arpine Engagement Photo, Aleppo, Syria: 1937.

Mosul, Iraq, 1939. Sarkis, Evelyn, Arlene, Rebecca holding Shakeh aka Ellen (front row left to right). Edward and Arpine (back row).

Mosul, Iraq, 1941. Evelyn, Rebecca & Arlene

American Photos

*Sometime between 1895 to 1900: Margaret Shamlian Geyikian
(sister of Toros Shamlian) and her Shamlian nephews in America.*

Roxie and Edward Shamlian, wedding photo, October 1948, San Francisco.

Mr. and Mrs. Yeranian wedding photo, 1945.

Rebecca Yeranian (nee Shamlian) and her husband, Arthur Yeranian, 1988.

Evelyn Shamlian Sarkisian & husband Sarkis,
Golden Gate Park, San Francisco, 1960s.

Arlene Shamlian Kazarian & husband Richard Kazarian.

Other Photos

Dicran and Armine Berberian, Europe, 1936.

Dr. Dicran Berberian, Lebanon, 1945.

ABOUT THE AUTHOR

Ellen Sarkisian Chesnut was born in Mosul, Iraq in 1939 and came to the United States at the age of two with her parents and baby brother on the *MS Boschfontein* to the Port of San Francisco, California.

Subsequently, she grew up and was educated in San Francisco, CA. She received a degree in teaching from San Francisco State College (now San Francisco State University) and taught in the San Francisco Unified School District [SFUSD] at the secondary level for forty-two years in the areas of Humanities, History, English, and Art. In 1995, she received the Visual Art High School Teacher Award from the SFUSD.

Ellen also became an accomplished artist specializing in printmaking, multi-media, and watercolor and has received awards for her works that combine memory and myth. Over the years she has shown her work in many shows and galleries: one woman show at the Nelson Morales Gallery in San Francisco in 1999, group exhibit at the Pacific Art League in Palo Alto, and exhibit in the San Francisco Women Artists' Gallery.

Most of all, Ellen throughout her life has been a student, lover, and enthusiast of Armenian culture and literature which in her 50s led her to write several non-fiction articles published in *ARARAT Quarterly*. Her first hand access to some unbelievable but true stories, heard from childhood onward, of the Armenian history of incremental genocides between 1894-1923 led her to seriously attempt collation and dissemination of these memories and knowledge to the larger public so as to be felt on a personal level, beyond a footnote in history books. To this end, she published her first book, *Deli Sarkis: The Scars He Carried*, in 2014 chronicling her father's journey as a first-hand witness to the Armenian genocides of the early 1900s. See www.scarshecarried.com and visit Ellen's YouTube channel—scarshecarried—to see videos.

Since her retirement from teaching in 2006, Ellen has dedicated herself to educating herself and helping others learn about Armenian culture which has remained vibrant and survives despite centuries of some of the most brutal genocides. She has also become the family archivist for both sides of her family and is the archivist of her late, beloved husband and fellow artist, Glen Earl Chesnut. Glen's family physical effects are currently at the Buffalo Bill Center of the West in Cody, Wyoming.

Ellen lives in the Bay Area of Northern California and enjoys gardening, current events, volunteering at the Alameda Naval Air Museum, working out at Total Woman Gym, and art of course! Follow her at www.ellensarkisianchesnut.com.

END NOTES

The Bloody Earth, 1894-1923

1. Jernazian, Ephraim K. *Judgment Unto Truth* (New Brunswick, NJ, Transaction Publishers, 1990), p. 8.

2. Balakian, Peter and Yaghlian, Nevart, Translators. *Bloody News from My Friend: Poems by Siamanto* (Detroit, Michigan, Wayne State University Press, 1996), p. 41-43.

3. Simonyan, Hrachik, translated by Brown, Melissa, and Zrzoumanian, Alexander. *The Destruction of Armenians in Cilicia, April 1909* (London, Gomidas Institute, 2012), p. 92.

4. Simonyan, Hrachik, translated by Brown, Melissa, and Zrzoumanian, Alexander. *The Destruction of Armenians in Cilicia, April 1909* (London, Gomidas Institute, 2012), p. 185.

5. Sarafian, Ara. "Talaat Pasha's Black Book." From the Armenian Report, 13 March 2009. Armenian Cause Foundation, PDF. www.armeniancause.net/wp-content/uploads/2009/04/N1-new.pdf.

Battle of Marash

6. Hartunian, Abraham H. *Neither to Laugh Nor to Weep,* 2nd Edition (Cambridge Mass., Armenian Heritage Press, 1986), p. 135.

Lydia Bagdikian

7. Bagdikian, Ben H. *The Memoir of Lydia Bagdikian* (Ben H. Bagdikian, Berkeley, California, 1997), p. 136.

BIBLIOGRAPHY

Akcam, Taner. *Killing Orders: Talat Pasha's Telegrams and the Armenian Genocide (Palgrave Studies in the History of Genocide)*. Gewerbestrasse, Switzerland: Palgrave Macmillian, 2018.

Altinay, Ayse Gul and Fethiye Cetin, translated by Maureen Freely. *The Grandchildren: The Hidden Legacy of "Lost Armenians in Turkey*. New Brunswick, New Jersey: Transactcon Publishers, 2014.

Bagdasarian, Adam. *Forgotten Fire*. New York: DK Publishing (Dorling Kindersley), 2000.

Bagdikian, Ben H. *Double Vision: Reflections on My Heritage, Life, and Profession*. Boston: Beacon Press, 1995.

Bagdikian, Ben H (editor). *The Memoir of Lydia Bagdikian*. Berkeley, California: 1997.

Balakian, Grigoris. Translated by Peter Balakian with Aris Sevag. *Armenian Golgotha: A Memoir of the Armenian Genocide, 1915-1918*. New York: Alfred A. Knopf, 2009.

Balakian, Peter. *The Burning Tigris: The Armenian Genocide and America's Response*. New York: Harper Collins Publishers, 2003.

Balakian, Peter. *Vise and Shadow: Essays on the Lyric Imagination, Poetry, Art, and Culture*. Chicago: University of Chicago Press, 2010.

Berberian, Dicran Abraham. *Dr. Dicran Abraham Berberian's Personal Papers*. Edited and transcribed by Raffi Berberian, Telma Trimmer, and Dr. Robert Whitfield Trimmer. Transcripts received by author in 2015-2016. Raffi Berberian: raffiberberian@gmail.com

Benoit, Monique. "Memories of the Heart," San Francisco Chronicle, December 1962.

Cetin, Fethiye. Translated by Maureen Freely. *My Grandmother: A Memoir.* London/New York: Verso, 2008.

Charentz, Yeghishe. Translated by David Kherdian and Garig Basmadjian. *13 Poems.* Glendale, California: Abril Publishing Company, 2008.

Dadrian, Vahakn N. *German Responsibility in the Armenian Genocide.* Watertown, Massachusetts: Blue Crane Books, 1996.

Dadrian, Vahakn N. *The History of the Armenian Genocide: Ethnic Conflict from the Balkans to Anatolia to the Caucasus.* Providence: Berghahn Books, 1995.

Dadrian, Vahakn N. *Warrant for Genocide.* New Brunswick/London: Transaction Publishers, 1999.

Derdarian, Mae M. based on a Memoir by Virginia Meghroune Vergeen. *Vergeen: A Survivor of the Armenian Genocide.* Los Angeles: Atmus Press Publications, 1997.

Eisen, Jonathan and Hale, Dennis. *The California Dream.* New York: The Macmillan Co., 1968.

Gingeras, Ryan. *Sorrowful Shores: Violence, Ethnicity, and the End of the Ottoman Empire, 1912-1923.* Oxford/New York: Oxford University Press, 2009.

Hagopian, Roger. *Memories of Marash. The Legacy of a Lost Armenian Community.* Copyright 2004. DVD by Yesnig Productions.

Hartunian, Abraham H. Translated by Vartan Hartunian. *Neither to Laugh Nor to Weep: A Memoir of the Armenian Genocide.* Cambridge, Massachusetts: Armenian Heritage Press, 1986.

Jernazian, Ephraim K. Translated by Alice Haig. *Judgment Unto Truth: Witnessing the Armenian Genocide.* New Brunswick: Transaction Publishers, 1990.

Jones, Maldwyn Allen. *American Immigration.* Chicago: University of Chicago Press, 1960.

Kerr, Stanley E. *The Lions of Marash; Personal Experiences with American Near East Relief, 1919-1922.* SUNY Press, 1973.

Kurt, Ümit. *The Curious Case of Ali Cenani Bey: the Story of Agénocidaire During and After the 1915 Armenian Genocide.* Patterns of Prejudice: 52:1, 58-77. DOI:10.1080/0031322X.2018.1430887 (Accessed: 01/03/19)

Kevork, Baboian. Translated and Introduced by Umit Kurt. *The Heroic Battle of Aintab.* Cleveland/London: Gomidas Institute, 2018.

Leverkeuhn, Paul. Translated by Alasdair Lean. *A German Officer During the Armenian Genocide: A Biography of Max von Scheubner-Richter.* London: Taderon Press for the Gomidas Institute, 2008.

Malcom, M. Vartan. *The Armenians in America.* Boston: The Palirim Press, 1919.

Nalbandian, Inga. Translated and edited by Victoria Rowe. *Your Brother's Blood Cries Out.* London: Gomidas Institute, 2007.

Panian, Karnig. Translated by Simon Beugekian. Goodbye, Antoura: A Memoir of the Armenian Genocide. Stanford, California: Stanford University Press, 2015.

Rowe, Victoria. *A History of Armenian Women's Writing, 1880-1922.* London: Taderon Press for the Gomidas Institute, 2009.

Sarafian, Ara. *"Talaat Pasha's Black Book Documents His Campaign of Race Extermination, 1915-17 " from the Armenian Report, 13 March 2009.* Armenian Cause Foundation: 2009. www.armeniancause.net/wp-content/uploads/2009/04/N1-new.pdf (Accessed: 01/03/19)

Saroyan, William. *My Name is Aram.* New York: Ilarcourt, Brace and World, Inc., 1937.

Shrikian, Gorun. *Armenians Under the Ottoman Empire and the American Mission's Influence on Their Intellectual and Social Renaissance.* Ottawa, Canada: UMI Dissertation Services, 2011. St. Sarkis Armenian Church in Detroit, Michigan, (313) 336-6200.

Siamanto. Translated by Peter Balakian and Nevart Yaghlian. *Bloody News from My Friend: Poems by Siamanto.* Detroit: Wayne State University, 1996.

Simonyan, Hrachik. Translated by Melissa Brown and Alexander Arzumanian. *The Destruction of Armenians in Cilicia, April 1909.* London: Gomidas Institute, 2012.

Walker, Christopher J. *Armenia: The Survival of a Nation.* New York: St. Martin's Press, 1980.

Western Paint Review. *Color Creativity... Keeps the Customers Coming.* Los Angeles, December 1968. (Article)

Yessayan, Zabel. Translated by G.M. Goshgarian. *In the Ruins: The 1909 Massacres of Armenians in Adana, Turkey.* Boston: Aiwa Press, 2016.

Zaroukian, Andranik. Translated by Elise Bayiaian and Marzbed Margossian. *Men Without Childhood.* New York: Ashod Press, 1985.

www.ingramcontent.com/pod-product-compliance
Lightning Source LLC
Chambersburg PA
CBHW021058090426
42738CB00006B/399